Managing 21st Century Libraries

Lyndon Pugh

The Scarecrow Press, Inc.
Lanham, Maryland • Toronto • Oxford
2005

SCARECROW PRESS, INC.

Published in the United States of America
by Scarecrow Press, Inc.
A wholly owned subsidiary of
The Rowman & Littlefield Publishing Group, Inc.
4501 Forbes Boulevard, Suite 200, Lanham, Maryland 20706
www.scarecrowpress.com

PO Box 317
Oxford
OX2 9RU, UK

British Library Cataloguing in Publication Information Available

Library of Congress Cataloging-in-Publication Data

Pugh, Lyndon.
 Managing 21st century libraries / Lyndon Pugh.
  p. cm.
 Includes bibliographical references and index.
 ISBN 0-8108-5185-7 (pbk. : alk. paper)
 1. Library administration. 2. Library personnel management. I. Title:
Managing twenty-first century libraries. II. Title.

Z678.P987 2005
025.1—dc22   2005014531

Contents

List of Figures   v
Acknowledgments   vii
Introduction   ix

Part 1: The Background and the Basics

Chapter 1   Contemporary Library Characteristics   3
Chapter 2   A Modern Perspective   23
Chapter 3   Structures   47

Part 2: Managing People in Contemporary Libraries

Chapter 4   Skills for Managing and Learning   77
Chapter 5   Leadership   99
Chapter 6   The Player Manager   117
Chapter 7   Motivation   133

Part 3: A Solution

Chapter 8   Some Team Issues   145
Chapter 9   A Team Model   177

Bibliography   197
Index   205
About the Author   211

Figures

1.1	Factors Influencing the Nature of Contemporary Libraries	21
2.1	A Conventional Information Services Structure	39
2.2	The Underlying Social Network	40
2.3	The Relationship between Conventional Management, Change, Diversity, and Ambiguity	44
3.1	The Hub and Spoke	63
3.2	The Circle	64
3.3	The Living Network	66
3.4	Structural Flexibility and Creative Friction	68
5.1	The Development of Influential Leadership	103
7.1	Roles and Responsibilities in Motivation	142
8.1	A Conventional Communications Process	154
9.1	The Distributed Team Model	183
9.2	A Team-Based Organization circa 1943	187

Acknowledgments

The ideas expressed in chapters 1 and 2 are developed from an address given at the Annual Conference of the Swedish Association of Information Specialists, Stockholm, 19th November 2002, and subsequently published in an extended version in the *Nordic Journal of Documentation* 58, no. 1, 2003. Some parts of chapter 3 are a reworking of themes initially explored at this conference and reported in the same issue of the journal. Chapter 3 leans very heavily on Verna Allee's work, cited in the text and the bibliography. Philip Auger and Joy Palmer had a seminal influence on chapter 6. Their ideas are present throughout the main argument of this book.

Chapters 7, 8, and 9 on distributed teams have been very much colored by the work on virtual organizations done by Lisa Kimball of Group Jazz (www.groupjazz.com) and on a paper produced by Chris Kimble, Feng Li, and Alexis Barlow of the University of Strathclyde Business School. Their influence extends throughout the chapter. Above all, chapter 7, and part of chapter 8, have been inspired by the writing of the late Sumantra Ghoshal and Christopher Bartlett; my debt to them is enormous.

The image on page 187 was taken by the late Arthur Gibson and is published with the kind permission of After the Battle and Image in Industry.

The apparently indiscriminate use of the terms hybrid library, electronic library, digital library, information services and library will infuriate the purists. They are used as shorthand for 21st century library services, and the variation in their use is simply an attempt to avoid repetition and boredom.

Introduction

This book is about encouraging a small outbreak of anarchy in the interests of organizational health. It is not about the technical aspects of managing libraries. It is nothing whatsoever to do with the processes of strategic planning, policy creation, budgeting, project management, or performance assessment. There are already a number of library management textbooks that cover these topics. The book is first of all about creating the circumstances in which people can use their talents to the full. It also has something to do with helping people to identify the things they are good at, match them with what the organization wants, and apply those skills in the interests of organization development and their own personal development. It is about creating opportunities for people to work with others in ways that engage all the abilities of everyone involved, and it is about developing an organization that is an interesting, stimulating, provocative, and effective place to work. Some recent unstructured interviews with a range of professional librarians in the UK (Pugh, 2004) indicated a considerable degree of interest in new ideas about library organization, although there was less evidence that these ideas were appearing in practice.

Above all, the book is about the ways in which library managers and staff can develop systems for managing contemporary library services, and take advantage of the unique combination of circumstances that provide the potential for innovative organization development in the library services of today. It specifically relates important issues in people management to the characteristics of libraries that deal significantly with both digital and printed material.

The genesis of the text can be traced to the confluence of a number of influences. The first of these is the view, formed over years of practical experience of management in libraries, and an involvement with managers in other sectors, that organizations and the people who work in them suffer from the debilitating consequences of overmanagement. Managing a library, whether it is a traditional one or a postmodernist one (whatever that really means), is a practical activity. It also seems to be an activity that is easily hijacked, and one of the consequences of this, which we cannot seem to shake off, is the continuing gulf between managing and doing. This adds significantly to the structural rigidity of organizations.

This did not matter while libraries were relatively stable organizations. Their management principles then were drawn from a set of tried and tested theories which were appropriate and effective for the times, and for library staff and users. Bureaucracy undoubtedly worked, but sadly it is alive and well at the beginning of the 21st century, when libraries are operating in markedly different conditions.

Tripsas, in an interview with Roberts (2004) called this type of traditional organizational form the "dominant design," which tends to breed a particular mind-set that restricts development, in particular development associated with radical technology such as digitization. As this is the key factor in current library services development, it should clearly be a factor in the way we organize libraries, but should go well beyond the purely technical, economic, and policy issues that tend to predominate in the literature. Digitization alongside conventional collections also represent fertile conditions for change in most aspects of organizational life.

The second factor that has influenced this book is the change in our understanding of how certain groups of people in the workforce prefer to work, and what kind of working conditions help them to operate at their optimum efficiency. Looking, even superficially, at the way in which knowledge workers, information technology experts, and others in the knowledge-related sector are organized, it is clear that they place a premium on self-directed activity, working in teams, and using initiative. The environments they operate in tend to be dynamic and abrasive, and this vigor stems from the juxtaposition of different talents, backgrounds, professional cultures, and ways of looking at things. Investigating the growth of these and other ideas, and practice in the wider world of general management, offers a number of clues as to how the task of managing modern information services can be approached.

We are also witnessing substantial changes in the skills and abilities of library staff as a group. Growing technological expertise and the broadening of managerial and operational portfolios to include areas like marketing and income generation, as well as the influence of increasing numbers of staff from other sectors, have increased the number of people in our organizations who have a predilection for working in the ways described in the previous paragraph. This change has been accompanied by shifts in user needs and in the approach of users to gathering information—seen most notably in an increasing technological competence that will eventually lead to some self-sufficiency in the identification and exploitation of stored knowledge.

Concurrently, the information services of today operate in circumstances that have never been more conducive to innovative organization development. These conditions are examined in chapter 1. There is also evidence to support the view that the profession has been slow to take advantage of these conditions, so this was another impetus behind this book. Over a number of years, various examinations of organization development, in particular the nature and implications of structural change (Pugh, 1990, 1997, 2002, 2004) identified a number of problems seen mainly in the evidence of

- Immature team development
- Functionally based service delivery
- Limited physical integration of services
- Predominantly hierarchical structures
- Excessive concentration of power at the top of organizations
- Undeveloped views on organizational learning, skills acquisition and transfer, and information sharing
- Little change in the important roles and functions of middle management

All of this tended to nullify the potential advantages of working with diverse staff groups in information services that themselves reflected considerable diversity that could be used as a creative force for development.

Roberts (2004) suggested that one of the vital factors in dealing with, and exploiting, the kind of technological change faced by organizations is to develop new perspectives. The dialog with Tripsas referred to above went on to advance the idea that changing the mental model of the organization depended on "adding key outsiders—who don't have the same history and the same biases—to the mix." Taking advantage of these "key outsiders," either present in the flesh or via their ideas, is part of the approach of this book. It is also obvious that some of the "key outsiders" are already in our organizations but are relatively unexploited.

Abrahamson (2004) developed the idea that today's organizational change could be managed through a reconfiguration of the basic components of the organizational architecture:

- People
- Networks
- Culture
- Processes
- Structures

> employees create networks . . . exchange information, favors, resources, and even gossip through the firm's informal systems . . . culture comprises its values (for instance, decision by consensus), norms and informal roles. . . . Processes are the recurrent activities . . . that enable a firm to transform inputs . . . into outputs. Structure refers to the organizational boxes, lines of communication and reporting, staffing, and control mechanisms.
>
> (Abrahamson, 2004)

Hopefully, the underlying themes of this book will reflect Abrahamson's concerns, and also those covered by Hammer:

- Redeploy existing talents
- Recombine people, networks, cultures, structures, and processes
- Do not start with a blank sheet—use what is already there in a different way
- Tinker and patch
- Ask some simple questions: What is needed to achieve the objectives? What is already in place?
- Challenge long-held assumptions

(2004)

Some of the other lessons that emerge from the literature referred to in this introduction are also relevant issues for modern library management. Changing the existing mind-set involves rediscovering the willingness to take ideas from outside library management. The models discussed later in the text reflect this approach, as does the discussion of the theoretical basis for what is proposed.

A key theme throughout this book is developed from the work of the 19th century English poet John Keats, who wrote of negative capability. For the poet, this was when "a man is capable of being in uncertainties, Mysteries, doubts, without any irritable reaching after fact & reason"

(Rollins, 1958). It seems to be that being in a state of uncertainty is the overwhelming characteristic of library organizations today, but there are ways in which this can be used to improve our organizations.

The theme of negative capability has been notably taken up by Simpson, French, and Harvey (2002), who apply it to concepts of leadership. It refers to the ability to live with a state of uncertainty and to benefit from acknowledging the limits of what one knows. The idea is applied to the development of leadership in the first instance. It also has a wide application in the kinds of organizations described in this book, where there are uncertainties, incongruities, and differences. In library management there sometimes seems to be a tendency to face uncertainty by reinforcing control. The power of negative capability is that it supports reflection and measured thinking. It will not work in bureaucracies (Simpson, French, and Harvey, 2002) because bureaucracies thrive on eliminating doubt, but in the right sort of organization it will release creative energy. If this book has an overall purpose, it is to present the characteristics of those organizations.

The comments above hopefully go some way to explaining why this book is about structures, which in the view of the author are one of the vital components in library management, leadership, communication, management behavior, and skills. They may also explain why a book on library management leaves out some of the topics referred to in the opening paragraph.

Lyndon Pugh
Pennant
Ceredigion
Wales
September 2005

Part 1

The Background and the Basics

Chapter 1

Contemporary Library Characteristics

In her book on how business knowledge has changed and expanded over the space of less than ten years, Allee (2003) might well have been writing about libraries and librarians when she said of contemporary organizations,

> Many of the same management words are still around but the surrounding language has evolved and expanded. Some familiar words have totally different nuances today, and we have a whole range of new ones to describe the digital world of business. Almost all our business and managing concepts have expanded, evolved into something else, or been replaced. Many of the old rules for creating value no longer apply. We now must pay attention to different things and learn new questions. Yet, for the most part, we are still paying attention to the same things we used to, especially when it comes to thinking about organizations. We pay attention to the center and ignore the edges. Our focus isn't really on business in general; it is on companies. . . . Stories about companies also focus on the center within that center—the CEO and the leadership team . . . organizations have become so slippery now. They keep moving, changing, and morphing into other forms. The edges are blurred and fuzzy, and seem to be spilling over into other organizations. It is getting harder to tell where one leaves off and another begins.

The last four sentences are of course not applicable to libraries in the way Allee meant. This is a pity. In some senses, if the edges really were blurred and fuzzy and spilled over into other organizations, then there would be less need to write a book like this. Of libraries, it can be said with confidence that as organizations they *should* have "become so slippery now," but they have not; they *should* have been "moving, changing, and morphing into other forms," but they have not; the edges *should* have been "blurred and fuzzy," but they are not. If indeed they seem to be "spilling over into other organizations" then we have done little to help the process along.

Among many other factors leading to change, Allee identifies the Internet and digital technology as two. In the library context, they are crucial areas, and what we should be searching for is a way of taking advantage of the conditions in which knowledge-based, creative organizations find themselves operating. It is these conditions in combination, stemming from the Internet and digital technology, that should not only be shaping our thinking about how we organize libraries in the 21st century, but should also be leading by now to some tangible changes on the ground. The challenge is to engage with a process of organizational development that will create library forms fit to exploit the emerging forces in organizational change. Griffiths (2003), in a review of the impact of digital technology on television, suggested that while the basic technology had not changed for over 40 years, the impact of digitization, over a short space of time, was considerable. For libraries, until the late '60s and early '70s when the use of computers for housekeeping techniques expanded, there had been no significant change for 100 years. The development of electronic information sources alongside conventional printed material, and the digitization of the mid-'90s onward, represent change of a markedly greater order than the early computerization efforts, and the impact is potentially huge. To take the maximum advantage from this situation, we need to base our approach to this period of organizational development on

- An understanding of the impact of digital technology on all aspects of the organization
- An acceptance that digital technology offers the chance of widespread organizational change
- An awareness that electronic information, largely a technologically determined change, also has social and human resource significance
- An acknowledgment that, for at least the medium term, libraries will be hybrid organizations, and that this in itself offers opportunities for a creative approach to organization design and development

For libraries, all this will represent a major shift, and it will undo centuries of library management theory. The task is no less than facing the challenges spelled out by Allee and others: understanding that new rules apply, asking new questions, doing things in ways that might not seem natural and instinctive when viewed in the light of traditional management norms. Even a cursory examination of the literature will indicate the problems in achieving this state.

In what amounts to an overview of the approach required for organizational survival, Brickley and others (2003) effectively provide a list of dos and don'ts. Applied to libraries, this offers a sobering set of directives:

- Move away from traditional organizational structures
- Dispense with functional organizations
- Adopt flatter organizational shapes
- Learn how to flatten management structures without losing control
- Adopt a process-based system
- Eschew narrow technical expertise, particularly when it is ring-fenced from other organizational areas that would in fact benefit from sharing it and could add to it
- Overtly link decision making and authority with knowledge, skills, and influence, rather than with hierarchical position
- Establish strong links between organizational change, recruitment, development, and motivation
- Attack organizational development through cross-functional teams

What we are suffering from today in library management is the preponderance of a traditional and conservative approach to management—an approach that is not going to create organizations fit for the e-future:

> The next two or three decades are likely to see even greater technological change than has occurred in the decades since the emergence of the computer, and also even greater change in industry structures, in the economic landscape, and probably in the social landscape as well.
>
> (Drucker, 2002)

Drucker's account of the successive waves of change that engulfed Western society after the Industrial Revolution contains a number of parallels concerning the emergence of new and unforeseen industries and services. Taking his inspiration from the emergence of moveable type, Martin Luther, and Machiavelli, ranging by way of the industrialization of the fishing industry to biotechnology, he amply demonstrates the unpredictability of what is to come.

At the center of managing what he terms the "Knowledge Revolution," Drucker rightly places the knowledge worker. In order to maintain the "mind-set that accepted—indeed, eagerly welcomed—invention and innovation," these workers will need to work in organizations that have systems and models that satisfy their values. They will need partnerships, and they will need new kinds of leadership. I doubt that Drucker had libraries in mind when he continued to say that there is every indication that we will attempt to "straddle the fence," and make the effort to manage in the new environment by using, as Allee suggested (2003), the old theories, structures, and models. Nevertheless, we seem determined to regress even further and subject the people who run our organizations to fairly stiff doses of highly conventional management, and make them suffer for it in the end. The most astonishing thing of all is that we are attempting to absorb the impact of the potentially huge changes in our libraries by allowing the shock to be taken by the bureaucratic systems used for well over a century. Our attention to the technology is magnificent, but it runs alongside an "inability . . . to look beyond the immediate problems associated with the technology" (Town, in Hornby and Clarke, 2003). While we are undoubtedly in the throes of a massive change project as far as the management of collections of information and library functions are concerned, there is little sign that we are yet engaging in the broad task of developing a theoretical base for the new organizational forms that will be needed to operate in the new technological environment. Nor are we are yet able to articulate a coherent view on how to manage what are still the most important elements—the knowledge workers or information workers.

What Libraries Might Look Like in the 21st Century

Our contemporary library organizations are not good at managing the e-future. Scanning the literature suggests that there is a debate going on about the electronic library, and almost all of it is being conducted on very restricted terms. There is an expansive and valuable research effort, much of which is led by practitioners, and this is pushing forward the boundaries of our knowledge of e-library technology. In some countries, the quality of the digital and e-library developments has a cachet for the information profession, in that it has become enmeshed with numerous governmental efforts to push forward the wired society. It is very likely that there has never been a more propitious time for radical change in library operations, as library services are arguably receiving an unparalleled degree of attention. This is partly because of the way they have embraced an all-pervasive technology that is linked with issues such as lifelong learning and e-government. It is also caused by the growing acceptance of the significance of the management of digital information in business and commerce. In some instances this has triggered and sustained government involvement. Unfortunately, the changes are not being prosecuted beyond the narrow confines of technology. So there is a downside, to be found first in the fact that developments are driven by technology. That the way this debate has developed is leading to a situation where Allee's "familiar words have totally different nuances today, and we have a whole range of new ones" (2003) is fairly evident. What is being suggested is that we pay far too much attention to the technology, and nothing like enough to the human dimension of managing and working in modern library services.

Technological Determinism

Dearnley and Feather (2001), in a well-argued assessment of the nature of the information society and where it is going, are skeptical about the view that current changes are technologically determined. In the strict sense this skepticism might well be justified. However, in the sense that the current recurring waves of change are driven by technology, dominated by technology, and tend to exclude detailed consideration of other factors, there can be little argument. Technologists are setting the agenda, and this is most marked in the predominance of technological issues in the literature and in the way in which our vocabulary is changing. The single most important example of a familiar word that currently has a different nuance is the meaning now attached to the word "management" itself. In the context of the contemporary library, it has become something to do with procedures like the technical processes of setting up and running portals and gateways, or the administrative tasks of managing Web content, to quote two examples. This kind of distortion has been accompanied by something that, to someone who is not a technologist, looks almost like willful obscurantism. Metadata, once described as "a description of a description," is a classic example. Knowledge management, not by any means new, and eagerly embraced by some but sometimes more memorably described in some of the literature in quite derogatory terms, is another example. Technological change of the order that libraries are experiencing needs to be described simply and unambiguously, if unfashionably so, or else it becomes an exclusive preserve of the technologist. It will fail if we ourselves fail to recognize the fact that electronic library services are not based on technical trickery alone. They impose particular working conditions, make new demands on skills, and not least offer opportunities for new kinds of organizations. These hold the promise of novel freedoms in the ways in which work is done and overseen. Unless we see this, we will reach the point where we manage information, and not people or organizations. The nexus between the functions of the e-library and the people-driven processes that deliver those functions is becoming weaker. In this key sense alone, the charge of technological determinism can surely be proven. This growing bias can only be arrested by a clearer understanding of the relationships between the characteristics of the emerging e-libraries and mainstream management issues. This should open up a debate on organizational structures, organization development, organizational behavior, and the human aspects of management in general.

The Mixed Economy

Whatever the views of the doctrinaire Web warriors, one of the greatest strengths of the e-future is that in real-life information services there will be a mixed economy. On the ground, users will continue to need, and want, access to information stored in a range of formats drawn from local, regional, national, and international collections. Describing the Learning Café project at Glasgow Caledonian University, Watson (2003) wrote,

> in addition to the group learning facilities in the café, users have access to 350,000 volumes and 2000 journal titles. Whilst many of these are online, some are not, and never will be. It is widely recognized that when it comes to access to information we are in a hybrid situation. No matter how quickly we digitize what we have, paper is likely to persist as an information medium for the foreseeable future.

Collier (in Andrews and Law, 2004) criticizes this view because it states the obvious, but scanning the literature suggests it may not be obvious to all that many practitioners.

This hybridity of information services in the future is the single most crucial element in designing the organization. We will need to continue to make provision for those who find electronic information uncongenial, inappropriate, or simply unworkable. The implication of user preferences in this area is that we will be seeking a kind of organization that accommodates all these preferences. Users will eventually not really care in what form the information they need comes, as long as it meets their requirements. They will not care, and ideally will not know, whether their information needs are being met by a librarian, an IT specialist, or someone else. This imposes on libraries a responsibility to integrate all forms of information at the point of access and use. The evidence so far is that many services are still organized in ways that maintain impenetrable barriers between conventional and electronic information. They separate information on the basis of form, and separate library staff on the basis of what is essentially a spurious division between librarians dealing with electronic formats and others dealing with conventional material. Unfortunately, this kind of specialization effectively shuts off a crucial type of development. This is to be found in the energy that could be released in organizations built to foster interaction between different traditions, skills bases, training and education, and cultural norms. It also immunizes the information services sector against the cross-fertilization of ideas that come from a creative approach to organization design in other sectors. The latter are sectors where the vigor of the e-environment as a seed bed for new ideas about managing is already attested to. In some sectors of management, the debate has moved well beyond technology and is giving rise to questions about the shape of e-organizations, how leadership will be exercised, where power will reside, how rewards will be decided, how communication will occur, and what sort of culture will best sustain new organizations.

For a long time it has been accepted that innovation and creativity come from abrasion and the bringing together of several different approaches. Yet in information services, the idea that capitalizing on differences can be the bedrock of organizational development is anathema. This prevails even when there has never been a more opportune time to follow the idea through as far as library management is concerned.

A snapshot of organizational structures in information services (Pugh, 2004) revealed that far too many libraries have structures that separate information forms that should be integrated, and enclose specializations that should be exposed to each other. Too many information services are bureaucratic and hierarchical. They are vertically divided into library divisions, electronic information divisions, computer services, media services and other sections. Each specialized section houses specialized personnel, has dedicated and specialized management, and sometimes runs discrete systems.

This is a total waste. Instead of operating a truly mixed economy, at least two information services run side by side. There are electronic information managers and electronic information librarians hedged in by traditional organizational boundaries. These inhibit them from bringing their skills, knowledge, and experience to bear on the information problems of a wide range of users. Along with this waste of talent come the kind of communication problems and human development problems that arise from rigid structures. The tragedy is deepened by the fact that the electronic information revolution has within itself the solutions to problems of organizational inflexibility. If there is ever to be a realization of the idea of presenting the "seamless web of information" to users, then it has to come from using the technology to create flexibility (see chapter 3) because the hybrid or mixed economy breeds differences, and these differences will represent an opportunity for dynamic organizational growth.

There is another problem that will be critical, and that is the question of whether the bureaucracy can support and nourish the kind of leadership that will be needed from library directors in the 21st century (see chapter 5). The associated issues will be how best to support leadership that

- Challenges accepted wisdom
- Looks to the future
- Fosters innovation

Arguably, hierarchical systems cannot do this.

Complexity

Complexity occurs when there are many variables and unknowns in an organization. It is not to be confused with something that is complicated. Most traditional library structures are complicated, but they are under-standable, in part because they were designed to deal in what once were certainties. They exist in the shape they do to eliminate the complexity which is foreign to conventional library organizations. Built as they were to deal with information in standard packages, libraries are arranged in a way that requires the intervention of a librarian trained in the organization of information in order to produce that information for users. Standardization is a key word, and protection against deviation, ambiguity, and fuzziness is assured. This protection comes from rules and regulations, specialization, a no-risk culture, strong hierarchies, and conventional line management. The only possible area of complexity in a traditional library arises from the rigid internal divisions that make it difficult to know what is going on in some other parts of the organization.

Nevertheless, understanding the nature of complexity and embracing it as an opportunity for growth are two of the keys to the design of contem-porary library organizations. These organizations will actually be able to profit from ambiguity and differences and make positive virtues of them as they become cornerstones of creativity.

The complexity of electronic libraries comes partly from the systems used to run them, partly from our currently inadequate attempts to create management structures for them, and partly from the way in which digital information is beginning to change the service ethos of libraries. This issue is not only related to the process of directly providing information for users.

It is also connected to the actual relationship between the library and those users who are themselves introducing complexity through the increasing diversity, and hence variation, in their information needs. They are also threatening to actually manage their information access themselves, and what complexity this will introduce.

Of equal significance, digital information is compelling changes in the political landscape, as cross-sectoral developments blossom and thrive. This again leads to variety and uncertainty, as we know less about our putative collaborators and how to deal with them. In turn there should be a premium on much more sensitive and skillful management practices than will be found in the traditional bureaucracies that prevail in many libraries.

Complex Technologies

Although some library computer systems are among the most sophisticated in the world, technology in this sense refers to any and all of the things that are done to make a library work. They could be paper systems, information technology systems, or a combination of both. By and large, traditional library organizations are good examples of routine technology in action: complicated but not complex. Most things are done the same way every time, every day, with little or no deliberate variation. By any measure of the degree of complexity in organizations, libraries have been routine in the way in which technology is applied.

Organizations based on routine technology are amenable to bureaucratic management, and the organizational form used by most libraries throughout the last two centuries and into the 21st has been well suited to the routine way that work has been done. Happily, technologists themselves might not be quite as amenable to bureaucratic management, and therefore this is beginning to change slightly. So while the nature of the work is altering, there is sadly scant evidence that structures are adapting, or that management styles are changing, to encompass working situations that are better suited to more flexible and imaginative ways of managing.

From other areas of activity, we also know that knowledge workers in general are more amenable to new styles of management. In the e-library, the area of reader services is likely to see the most profound of all changes in this respect, as a result of what is described next. The big question is whether organizations will change their forms in step with this development, or whether they will continue to cling to the outdated but comfortable way of working they know today.

Personalization

Within the professional careers of some of the current generation of elder statesmen of librarianship, collection management has evolved significantly. It is still, but only just, possible to remember a time when many university libraries attempted, not always wholly successfully, to collect everything that was relevant to their teaching and research programs, whether it was used or not. This has been labeled "Just in case" collection development.

When economic realities started to bite, the phrase "Just in time" was applied to a situation where resources were acquired when they were needed—optimistically just before they were needed, in reality anything up to two years after. Collection management is now hovering on the cusp of the "Just for you" stage. This is where the real potential for change in library services actually lies, with the development of distributed information sources, access to local and distance information sources via the Web, Internet, Intranet, Extranet, and the availability of other electronic media. At its most refined, this process now allows for the possibility of providing a personalized service that combines the content of Web resources, remote databases, datasets, multimedia formats, electronic books and conventional printing. The increasingly wide range of library portals now in existence links access to library catalogues, Internet and Intranet search engines, e-journals, and internal databases. All of these add considerably to the scope and richness of a library's own resources, and they can be delivered to the desktop of the user, in a personalized form, with a choice of document delivery options. Information can come as full text, electronic abstracts, pdf documents, or images. Some of these portals work across sectors, integrating the resources of libraries, museums, and archives. At the next level up, there are projects with the bold purpose of setting up portals that form part of a national information structure. Employing standard software, it is now within the power of individual library users to effectively build their own personal libraries of which we as librarians might know little. Even in the softer areas of management, IT systems and software are beginning to have an impact (see chapter 9 for a discussion of team management software). What the new system cannot do is function without librarians (but see chapter 9), yet the role, function, and organization of librarians in this environment are neglected aspects of management.

The idea of the personalized library is a portent of how the control of this process of "Just for you" collection development and management is beginning to shift towards the users—users who are increasingly able to navigate their own way around this resource map. Elizabeth Burge, in her contribution to *Libraries Without Walls* (Brophy et al., 2002), called this "disintermediation,"—a disastrous moment for simple English. This can be taken to mean the removal of the librarian as the gatekeeper of information. She may not be the first to use this term, but the development itself is a long-predicted change:

> It is now within the power of the individual teacher or the department to control access to information themselves, and the pre-eminent role of the librarian as the unique gatekeeper is in question . . . [leading to] the emergence of various forms of instructional technology as rivals to the library.
>
> (Pugh, 1990)

The way this is playing itself out is welcome. The prospect of more library users becoming self-sufficient in analyzing their information needs, and retrieving relevant material in any format, is ultimately desirable:

> As central as the guide function has always been in the past, it's important to remember that our ultimate goal as librarians is to abdicate that role. We want our patrons to be able to find the information they need without our help. . . . If we think that nothing can beat a good librarian at helping patrons find good, relevant information, we are almost certainly wrong—and if we aren't wrong today, we will be tomorrow.
>
> (Curtis, 2002)

In the context of this book, the modification of the relationship between librarian, user, and information source in this way also has a more obvious significance. It is the real challenge in the design of library organizations for the future. The idea of massed battalions of users busily creating their own personal information portfolios might be a little far-fetched at present, but it only needs to happen on a small scale to create real organizational complexity, and it is not going to be easy to manage libraries working on this basis in the future. This is particularly true because until now libraries have been very strong on uniformity and very weak on differentiation. The weight of tradition and the inbuilt inertia of the bureaucracy are therefore against us, and the task of harnessing this complexity, and making sense of it, will be made more difficult if libraries still continue to creak under the burden of traditional structures and conventional hierarchical forms.

Specialization and New Skills

Electronic developments are producing their own skills specializations.

It might be possible to look askance at some of these specializations, but the process is now unstoppable. The difficulty does not arise exclusively because of the new skills that are needed, and the argument for some of these skills is overstated. The new lingua franca also conceals the fact that they are sometimes the old skills with new labels. Yet the larger difficulty is caused by the way the new specializations are accommodated within our organizations. Because information is on the Web, on a CD, or digitized, it is treated as a specialization in itself. Content managers organize it; metadata and Dublin Core are developed to describe it; knowledge managers oversee everything, although once upon a time everybody was a librarian. The problem is that this use of a new language, or attributing new meanings to features that have always been present and have not greatly changed (Allee, 2003), is only the most obvious manifestation of the way innovative developments in library services are currently handled. To repeat an earlier point, even the most superficial examination of the literature reveals that once the spotlight moves away from the technology and starts to pay lip service to "softer" management issues, the exegesis reveals no more than conventional information management (see, for example, Chowdhury and Chowdhury, 2003). The charge is that the approach now in vogue ignores much that is already widely known about complex, technologically driven organizations:

> The point about the actual management of digital libraries, like all other technologically dependent organizations, is that they will set totally different problems for managers, and should inspire new approaches to organizational design, development, and management.
>
> (Pugh, 2003a)

As already suggested, in practice electronic resources are frequently treated as a separate part of the library. Sometimes there are two systems, two managers, and effectively two libraries concealed within divisional forms: one housing conventional material, and one housing electronic or digital information.

There has never really been a case for locking specializations up in rigidly divided and hermetically sealed parts of the organization in any event, and there is much less of a case for doing this with the e-library. The survey referred to earlier (Pugh, 2004) confirmed the findings of research in 1990 (Pugh), 1997 (Pugh), and 2002 (Pugh): There is a preponderance of conventional and traditional management in libraries, and the favored way of dealing with electronic information is by giving it some degree of specialized treatment. There is no better illustration of this than the recent emergence of access services as yet another electronic specialization, a "product of the modern era of library automation" even though it is admitted that the "business of providing access to information resources is the most enduring and traditional of all library services" (Sapp, 2002). This writer sees access services as a

> third and equal partner in a model of a generalized sequence of a library's information handling services. First, technical services staff acquire and organize information so that it may be retrieved. Second, in a prototypical transaction, reference librarians assist the user to identify needed information. Finally, access services completes the cycle by either making the information package available to the user, or obtaining it on behalf of the user.

Thus an entirely function-based bureaucracy is perpetuated, and there is not much seamlessness here.

Modern library services will be staffed by librarians and by people from disciplines and walks of life outside the boundaries of professional librarianship: technologists, teachers, graphic designers, multimedia specialists, and people who fit into no particular professional group at all. The policy of appointing nonlibrarians to the highest library management posts in the land is not unknown, and there is little evidence that the results it produces are invariably significantly worst than those on offer when professional librarians are appointed. This is not the place to open up debates on the nature of management and specialist expertise versus management skills, but the previously unthought-of heresy of admitting managers from outside the sector to managerial posts in mainstream information services is already being committed. Sometimes it is also producing refreshing results in terms of a cross-fertilization of ideas from other sectors.

Nevertheless, even where the benefits of this cross-fertilization become clear, what is learned about making use of the perspective and specializations of others is not transferred into internal organizational arrangements. If there is a benefit to be gained at the top, why dilute this by setting up what are to all intents and purposes discrete organizations within organizations (see chapter 3). Managers thinking conventionally keep the different specializations apart and lose the potential organizational synergy that comes from bringing together different disciplines, traditions, training, and education. There is also much to be gained by observing and comparing different ways of looking at things. "Management is management is management" is a chant worth repeating if it underlines the need for us to learn from how other professions operate in the information economy.

The mind-set behind this version of specialization needs to be addressed. Two of the most invigorating developments in librarianship are first the dawning realization that there really will be "libraries without walls"—information will be increasingly delivered to remote users. The other is the influx of professionals from other sectors. Yet a Delphi Report (2002) indicated that while 91 percent of respondents felt that over half of library services would be delivered to remote users within ten years, only 44 percent of respondents felt this was desirable. Contrast this with Curtis's views (2002) and the distance to travel becomes clear.

Reactions to these changes are also illuminating. Dale (2002) referred to the "roles and responsibilities that [the profession] has given up to other professions over the last few years" in the corporate sector, and advocates ways of fighting back and reclaiming this lost influence and responsibility. The creative alternative to this response is to accept the responsibility of working with other professions as a way of creating effective e-libraries. It is also a way of developing the portfolio of skills, attributes, and experience necessary for library development in an age when the differences and the divisions between the information services professions and others will become indistinct, and the boundaries will hopefully be wholly porous. This is a healthier approach than the alternative of extending the competitive and ownership-based preoccupations of the bureaucracy into the 21st century.

Thinking about what can be learned from others will help make sense of the bewildering, almost complete uncertainty about the overall skills portfolio we will need. This is a counterbalance to the monolithic certainty of tradition and the zealotry of technology.

Sometimes, when the skills issue is addressed, massive lists of impossible attributes are drawn up, and this catchall approach can only deepen the sense of uncertainty and confusion. We are in fact no longer completely sure what skills a librarian will need in a digital environment. In this kind of confusion, seeking refuge in the deceptive verities of technological processes is understandable. Unfortunately, it goes hand in hand with an unwillingness to acknowledge that there should be an even stronger reliance on some of the traditional skills. The demands made by electronic library services on crucial human skills can be as heavy as those made by traditional library services. How, for example, will not being able to see the person asking the question affect a reference librarian working in a remote reference service when so much of communication depends on body language? Libraries will continue to deal with those activities

not conducive to the Web environment: a face-to-face meeting place, a cultural center, a place to collaborate on the development of educational technology, and a place to use the resources that must stay in the library.

(Curtis, 2002)

If the overemphasis on technology is bad for organizational design, then conversely the fact that new skills are being brought into the sector with the migration of new, noninformation service professionals is a positive spur to organizational creativity. It can no longer be said that librarianship is based on a discrete set of skills and a distinctive body of knowledge and expertise—if indeed it was ever conclusively so—but this is again an opportunity and not a threat. Equally, some of the conventional skills will become even more important alongside the task of mastering new technological skills. Adding all of these skills to the portfolio of essential talents needed by librarians, without making nonsense of their learning and training, is part of the task of organization development. The literature reflects a growing awareness of a continued need for conventional or traditional skills that are still relevant in the digital library world, such as the ability to write clearly and concisely even when engaged in the delivery of electronic reference services. It also reflects some concerns about the changes in skills requirements for catalogers and highlights a continuing need for staff working exclusively in electronic services to retain the interpersonal skills that provide the foundation for proper interaction with the public. A sober analysis indicates a continuing requirement for the skills built up by librarians over many years.

The list of skills needed, traditional and novel, but including many human resource management skills (Pugh, 2004), could be endless and will include

- Partnership skills—working with people who would not normally have been colleagues: those from different work cultures, with different priorities, different ways of doing things, different education and training backgrounds
- Collaborative skills—essential for cross-sectoral developments and working with erstwhile competitors
- Entrepreneurial skills
- Learning how to flatten management structures without losing control
- Change management skills

This combination of skills will not only create the appropriate environment for modern libraries, it will also actively encourage risk-taking and iconoclastic thinking . . . librarians have not generally been rewarded for coming up with and implementing crazy ideas. This will have to change.

(Curtis, 2002)

If the first obstacle to this is traditional thinking, as reflected in our insistence on applying the conventional tenets of librarianship to the 21st century library, the other one is structural.

Complex Structures

The two-systems approach to managing libraries has already been tried, and failed. It was used to deal with the growth of what were variously called audiovisual resources, nonbook resources, and more accurately multimedia that were habitually treated as special collections. The legacy of this mistake lasted for many years until most, but not all of us learned the value of integrated collections. The mistake is now being repeated, but probably with more serious consequences. Welding an electronic information division onto a conventional bureaucratic structure not only means that specialisms are kept apart. It leads to poor communication between the divisions, a lack of information about what is going on, no cross-fertilization of ideas, and a failure to effectively apply expertise to the needs of the user. This again is complexity, and as long ago as 1979, the argument was producing a potent brew. In that year Gorman, for example, examined the possibility of eliminating technical services altogether. This has not happened, but should have. Yet Gorman's words still resonate. He talked of the "absurd and damaging idea that there are public services types and technical services types" and although he never used the word "teams" he did use words like "seamlessness" and called for a "rounded understanding of the totality of librarianship." He coupled this appeal with a proposal to abolish hierarchies and ended with a reference to a "multidimensional library . . . [with] loose and more complex relationships between groups and persons." Almost 20 years later Bucknall (1996) attacked the equal folly of concentrating IT knowledge within one department. He argued that it led to a similar "polarisation of the library's knowledge base." Not only that, it inhibits skills acquisition and stands in the way of the application of these skills.

It has never been clear why the unrivalled knowledge of the collections held by catalogers should be retained within cataloging departments instead of being deployed where it really counts, in reader service and reference areas. It is even less clear why this should be so in the wall-free, barrier-removing electronic environment. Many systems librarians are expert project managers: Why lock this knowledge up? Why, in any event, allow the systems librarians to work exclusively on library systems that should actually require a far smaller input of staff time than they often luxuriate in?

These are obviously sweeping generalizations. There are some excellent examples of library services based on organic, team-centered structures. Skills are applied wherever necessary across the board, information flows freely through the organization, and management has at its disposal a range of behaviors and tactics well beyond traditional command and control. Yet they are exceptions.

Electronic information services call for a new approach. The effect of trying to fit them into a rigid bureaucratic system is debilitating. It has a deleterious impact on skills development, and it is not conducive to the attitude change that will be necessary in the digital library.

Not the least reason for asserting this is that the old structures are based on a principle which is anathema to the hybrid world. This world is one of collaboration, cooperation, and making the most of differences. As already hinted at, bureaucracies by contrast thrive on the idea of competition. This could be for resources, for individual promotion, for influence, for political power. It could be competition between line and staff management; between parts of the organization that are usually tied in to ideas about territory, and between individual managers who major in proprietorship. In the electronic world, boundaries are coming down; obtaining and using information no longer relies on institutional ownership but on access. The idea of ownership is out of date. Instead, many developments depend on alliances and working with new partners both within and outside institutions. Negotiation and collaboration are key management skills, alongside the development of new technological skills, and together with the use of entrepreneurial skills to develop the commercial aspects of library organizations and to prosecute innovation.

Competition

In almost every imaginable way, it can be said that libraries have existed within a comfortable consensus. There was a broad degree of agreement that they were a reasonably good thing—give or take the odd authoritarian government. Within the profession there was a fairly strong consensus on how things should be done, and why things were done in certain ways. There was virtually no significant competing provider of information. Some of this has already started to change as commercial information providers are moving into the market, sometimes alone and sometimes in collaboration with traditional providers. The rest of it will have to change because of the impact of the issues already discussed here—complexity, personalization, and unpredictability. The challenge of competition will have to be faced alongside the need for greater collaboration inside the library sector and across sectoral boundaries.

The result is the need for a different kind of organization: one that is good at innovation, able to change direction quickly, able to rapidly develop new ways of presenting information, able to develop new roles for its staff, and able to produce managers who think differently. There will be a call for organizations that will develop the information and learning systems that equip them to deal with all these changes.

Unpredictability

The essence of the environment in which e-libraries will operate is unpredictability. Much of the information landscape is unpredictable because of the volatility of the Web, the unstructured nature of certain aspects of the digital information world, the complicated world of access rights, and even things like changes in the nature of browsing behavior.

In some quarters it is argued with some force that browsing, that most unpredictable of all user behaviors, is one of the most important ways in which users acquire information. How much do we really know about how to deal with this in the e-library? What will users do without it? We know little enough of it in the conventional library.

Add to this the difficulty of planning for technological change which cannot be foreseen and the uncertainty surrounding the skills base. Compound the situation by considering the inappropriateness of present organizational forms, the hybrid nature of information itself, and the collapse of the old professional boundaries, allowing the entry of other professions and demanding partnerships and collaboration, and the uncertainty of the environment is then obvious.

There is now a clear approach to handling volatility in organizations:

- Change the mind-set. Accept volatility as a force for creativity and harness it
- Decentralize the organization, pushing authority, accountability, and power as far down the structure as possible
- Harness structural change, making organizations flatter, strengthening lateral communications and shortening vertical ones
- Develop multiple leaders with new leadership styles
- Build an organization around the learning, behavior, and attitude change that must be vital in an e-library context

The manner in which the influences described in this chapter interact and affect the organization of library services is shown below. The implications of each of these issues and their interrelationships are discussed in this chapter.

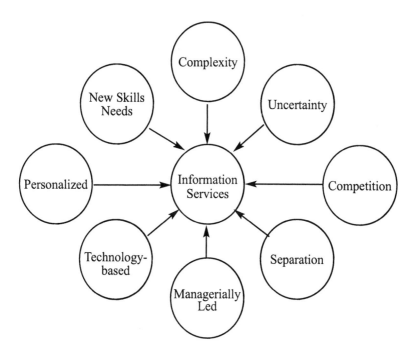

Figure 1.1 Factors Influencing the Nature of Contemporary Libraries

Summary

The library of the 21st century is going to develop into something very different from the libraries that served their clienteles reasonably well throughout the centuries dominated by printed information. It is going to be characterized by

- Technology-driven change
- Combinations of print and electronic media

- Technological complexity
- Complex user behavior because of the personalization of information
- Unpredictability
- Openness and responsiveness to competition
- New concepts of leadership and management skills
- Collaboration
- Open information systems
- Structures and procedures that make the best use of all the available human talents

This amounts to the adoption of large-scale organization development.

Chapter 2

A Modern Perspective

The first chapter illustrated the difficulty encountered in formulating ideas about contemporary library management, with a picture of a unique combination of factors that should, at least in theory, alter totally the information service manager's approach. If we start where we finished with the first chapter, we have a list of characteristics of contemporary libraries:

- Powered by technology
- Housing print, conventional multimedia, and various forms of electronic and digital media
- Delivering resources to distant users, and providing access to distant resources for their own users
- Complex in terms of the use of technology, and complicated in terms of their organizational structures. There is no better illustration of the frightening complications of some contemporary library organizations than some of those reported in Clegg (2003).
- Dealing with users in possession of a higher degree of information-seeking expertise than hitherto
- Using electronic resources that might be transient and therefore difficult to control
- Facing competition in the provision of information
- With a need to develop collaboration with other providers
- Deploying a combination of traditional and new skills
- Managing staff from outside the conventional information worker tradition, training, and education
- Using some staff who might be more aware of the possibilities of self-

management and empowerment
- Working on principles that were designed for different operating conditions, when the environment and the organization were more stable

The major question is where we should look for a theoretical framework capable of offering guidance when most of our ideas about the basis of organizational design come from more comfortable times of certainty and conformity. The difficulty also lies in the fact that while we might well have intellectually accepted ideas about teams, empowerment, decentralization, and new organizational structures, sometimes even positively embracing things like knowledge management, it does not show to any great extent in practice (Pugh, 1990,1997, 2002, 2004).

It is possible to see this conservatism as a fairly consistent strand in library management thinking, reflected in most of the standard texts on library management over the last 20 years (see, for example: Lynch, 1985; Bryson, 1999; Schmidt and Rieck, 2000; even Stueart and Moran, 2002, where the thrust of the work is on formal structures, specialization, and coordination). The last but one of these, being a tract on the management of media services, where innovative ideas about integrative management might be assumed to lurk, is the most surprising. Yet I suppose it should be admitted, albeit grudgingly, that conventional management has served libraries well. It should also be acknowledged that the canons underlying scientific management, bureaucracies, and Fayol's administrative management (1971), for example, could continue to provide a framework for the competent but unimaginative administration of modern-day libraries. It is impossible to prove that any system of management is more effective than any other, but whether conventional ideas will provide organizations that make the best of all the resources at their command is another matter.

The Library Organization as a Machine

Classical management theory, often described as an attempt to find the "one best way of managing," and broadly embracing the trends identified earlier, established a number of characteristics considered essential to good management in all sectors. From the scientific school, we find

- Systematic planning
- Rewards based on results
- Group working, ostensibly leading to teamwork
- Maximum throughput of standardized production

Some writers would see in this list a few desirable characteristics for modern library services, and nobody would argue about the relevance of planning, or the idea of teamwork. Other writers point out that while Taylor might well have sold his theories as beneficial developments for workers, in practice they were all about reducing the worker's room for using initiative, concentrating authority at the top of organizations, and control. David K. Carr (1996) in what is still one of the best available books on the practical process of change management, is only one expert who refers to the weight of the influence of military management on early management theory. It is of course true that many of the principles upon which library management was based up to the end of the 20th century, and beyond, can be traced back to the army of ancient Rome. Continuous production lines, turning out identical products based on standardized parts, were used to build Phoenician galleys because there was no other way of meeting the heavy demand created by losses to piracy (Morgan, 1997). Henry Ford's automobile production lines reflected the continuous lines of carcasses hanging from hooks in late 19th and early 20th century Chicago slaughterhouses. Early ideas in the military sphere were further refined by Frederick the Great of Prussia and others. These all embody something of bureaucratic management, and modern library services reflect this not only operationally but also in the use of language: span of control, chain of command, line management, unity of command—all reminiscent of the military sphere, and what the bureaucratic school brought to management theory is very much a refinement of the discipline that already existed, seen in

- Hierarchical management
- Activities based on formal rules
- Specialization
- Specific tasks and responsibilities for each worker
- Separation of line and staff management
- Discipline and control
- Clear lines of communication
- Clarity of management authority—only one boss in each area
- Clear boundaries within the organization
- The affirmation of management's responsibility for managing

It is somewhat unfortunate that we have not followed through on some of the more imaginative and expansive changes in military management, automobile manufacture, and manufacturing processes in other areas outside these examples (Pugh, 2000). The present basis for managing libraries has endured for most of the history of library organizations, and it obviously reflects a general view of the organization as a machine. What was lacking in this approach was an adequate emphasis on what some later commentators called the "softer skills" of management.

A Machine Run by People: Human Relations

Leadership, influence, collaboration, group dynamics, motivation—the absence of any real allowance for these issues typifies the weaknesses of the bureaucratic approach not only in the present context, but also in its heyday. The broad swathe of human relations theory attempted to rectify this by emphasizing the human element in managing organizations. Motivation and employee satisfaction were the key, and a totally different way of managing emerged as a result. This was based in part on

- The general significance of groups in the workplace
- The influence of informal leaders and informal groups
- The dynamic involvement of management

Unfortunately there has been no widespread adoption of these ideas in library management. What has happened is that the bureaucracy has been softened up around the edges without really shifting the emphasis in areas that are significant for organizational change. This is equally true of the practical impact of later ideas about systems theory, contingency theory, knowledge management, organization development, and learning organizations. We have also been slow to embrace the adoption of new organizational models that have featured in the thinking of contemporary management theorists outside information services. It is arguable that these strands in management thinking offer much more to modern libraries than the classical approach, but the practice, as opposed to the theory, has hardly developed beyond the bureaucracy.

There are some notable departures from this rule, but in general we have been left with an unenviable legacy as the electronic library emerges in mainstream information services. We adhere to theories and models that were ideal for the libraries of the 19th century, and perhaps for much, but not all, of the last century. These were appropriate for libraries that possessed a number of characteristics that made them prime candidates for classical management approaches.

Operating within a Consensus

This has probably been the single most important factor that has shaped the library profession's attitude to change up to the present time. The relationship between a traditional library, its parent organization, its staff, its users, and any other stakeholders, is one between consenting adults. It is not an exaggeration to say that for most of the time there has been broad agreement about what a library should do, how it should be done, and what it should not do. Technological developments offer us an opportunity to apply contrasting, new, and more appropriate models to library services operating in the 21st century.

Functionally Based

The delivery of library services has predominantly been based on the efficient organization of basic functions: acquisitions, cataloging, processing and organizing material, lending services, and reference services. These have been the life systems of the library, as well as representing a solid and relatively easily managed way of delivering services to users. Any expansion involved an effort to adopt new forms by instinctively scarfing and brazing new specializations onto an existing organization that some people would say was already creaking when the electronic library was nothing more than a glint in some technologist's eye. This is, after all, the way we have dealt with all forms of nonbook material, and here I deliberately avoid the use of the correct term "multimedia" in order to emphasize the stereotypical and unimaginative approach. It is also the way that we are trying to deal with electronic information. In spite of the lip service sometimes paid to teams and other forms of structural change, the kind of specialization and separation embodied in the tradition is still fairly typical on the ground.

Classical Perfection

Libraries have in some ways been classical bureaucracies. They have been very good at putting a maximum amount of work through a system that is designed to deal with a standardized product. They have done this with the aid of a controlled workforce. This workforce toils within a framework of rules that would have pleased those earlier centralists, the emperors of the Ming Dynasty. That was before they collapsed under the weight of paper the system produced, and the power of the Manchus. Libraries reflect a division of work, specialization, authority, communication, and managerial roles.

Contemporary Imperfection

Indubitably, this conservative approach produced administratively competent management of efficient organizations, in line with the 19th century definitions of efficiency and competence. What it largely failed to do is implant and sustain a managerial turn of mind that would incubate organizations preparing for the electronic future. Equally important, it hardly led to organizations that were fitted out and conditioned to deal with changes occurring well before electronic libraries grabbed the attention. The latter part of the 20th century saw changes in the way that librarians were educated and trained, and the development of a more sophisticated approach to workplace learning. In some countries it also reflected an increasing, and for once benevolent and positive, involvement of government in library issues. This process has led to electronic library programs. These in turn stimulated moves toward the creation of national information networks that often involve cross-sectoral collaboration and an increasingly heavy financial commitment to information technology in libraries. Lankes and others (2003) argue that in the United States at least, there is now equality between the use of conventional and digital resources. Similar perspectives have emerged in other parts of the world, and recent contact with library managers in Argentina uncovered a growing interest in the merging of academic support services in universities, reflecting one of the consequences of the Follett Report (1993) that led to a new focus on the nature of university libraries in the UK.

A less tangible result of the changes that accompanied the onset of electronic information was a change in expectations. Even before considering the implications of working in technologically driven organizations, library staff—better educated, with better access to training and development, and a shrewder understanding that information provision and management was becoming more important—might well have felt slightly uncomfortable in organizations that were in some ways almost schizophrenic. On the one hand they were offered a narrow specialization, bound by regulations and reward systems derived from an earlier age, hampered by a lack of wider awareness, and tied to a conventional career path. On the other, they saw a more exciting prospect of working with cutting-edge technology. How would people feel about working within the famous classic hierarchical pyramid—with its carefully delineated strategic, controlling, and operational levels—while, by the mid-1990s at the latest, mainstream management outside the library world was beginning to display at least some cognizance of exciting new organizational shapes? These hinted at dismantling hierarchical levels, blurring the distinction between strategy and operations, and broadening the inputs into strategy and policy formulation. As suggested here, ideas in the Follett Report (1993) went some way toward sketching out broad organizational characteristics that would have better equipped contemporary library managers for the task of creating organizations that made the best use of technology. These ideal organizations would also have provided the basis of a vibrant hybrid library service that utilized all resources, including the human ones, to the full.

Systems Theory

One of the abiding ironies suggested on the previous page is that while libraries might have been umbilically linked to classical management, in other sectors the weaknesses of this approach were giving rise to a number of ideas that, taken as a whole, would have laid down a strong base for the electronic services of the 21st century.

We might speculate on why intellectually and philosophically attractive ideas about management seem to have received scant attention from a practical point of view. Theories discussed in the rest of this chapter have a pedigree stretching back in some cases to the early 1950s, and team organizations in other areas predate even that. There are many models for the innovative management of digital libraries, and not much that is new in the appropriate theories.

Systems theory, or open systems theory, is but one example. It argues that the organization is a system which operates within both a formal and informal dimension. Organizational health and success will depend on the interplay and communication between the formal and informal system, and between the various subsystems that make up the whole. Burnes (2004) put forward a useful breakdown of the subsystems that might be found in an information service:

- The skills, processes, and knowledge of the protagonists
- Values, as represented by aims and objectives
- Culture
- Management systems
- Structures—ultimately a major factor that determines the nature of most of the other systems

While it could be added that the single most important factor in deciding how an organization is managed is the personality of the manager (see chapters 5, 6, and 7), it is important at this stage to accept that there is a vital interplay between all the subsystems, irrespective of the manager's personality. Developments or changes in one area have an impact on all of the others. This impact depends essentially on the levels of informal communication and cooperation that emerge in all organizations, as well as the formal collaborative mechanisms. Not only should the boundaries between the subsystems be completely permeable, but the boundary between the organization and its wider environment should also be open. This openness means that relevant changes in the circumstances surrounding and influencing organizations can be monitored. Threats and opportunities can then be identified, and organization development can occur.

It is not correct to suggest that there is a great deal of internal permeability to be found in the functional organization and the well-marked boundaries of traditional libraries. Although one of the interesting findings in a previously mentioned small-scale research project (Pugh, 2004) was the predominance of the management view that horizontal communication in library organizations was at least as strong and effective as vertical communications, this tended to be contradicted to some extent by other observations during the same piece of research.

Systems Theory, which emphasizes cross-boundary communication, is a good way of conceptualizing the modern library service. It is appropriate for an environment in which the idea of a physically delineated library becomes less relevant: As access to remote resources becomes at least as significant as building physical collections; as ICT-competent users control more of their own information-seeking activities; and as competition and alternative sources for the provision of information become more widespread. While it is not a complete solution to the design problem, it is a sound starting point, rooted as it is in the Field Theory of Kurt Lewin (1952), where the effect of a change in any part of an organization is seen to disturb the equilibrium and spread throughout the entire organization.

Organization Development

Bringing together both the human relations school and systems theory, Organization Development (OD) provides a valid, but not necessarily complete, template for the development of electronic libraries. It also introduces an additional element that should be characteristic of today's information services, and that is the importance of creating organizations that capitalize on the ability of individuals to learn. Given the problems surrounding the skills issue, this is now crucial. Allied to it is the need for individuals to take responsibility and to grow professionally. This has to be matched by the readiness of management to engage in behavioral change, to think differently about the way jobs are organized, and to prosecute the kind of structural change that makes all these things possible. Therefore, while OD has sometimes been primarily seen as an approach to change management, it succinctly brings together many ideas that should feature in modern, technologically complex organizations:

- Team structures to improve learning
- Flexible structures
- Job redesign
- Flexible leadership and management styles

OD is about changing attitudes . . . refocusing people's perceptions of the organization they work in. . . . improving communication and interaction through new structures and through the informal patterns which underpin structures . . . the organization is making the best possible use of all its resources and talents. It is also increasing its knowledge base as its staff learn about themselves . . . [and] their environment.

(Pugh, 2000)

Libraries as Learning Organizations

There is little doubt that libraries should have been a fertile breeding ground for the theory of learning organizations. Like most of the innovative management thinking of the late 20th century, it largely passed us by. When we consider the needs of the emerging electronic libraries, the idea has much to say that is relevant. It is also true that the corpus of knowledge that surrounds this particular theory has moved on, and to a degree been overtaken by other ideas. Given the putative characteristics of electronic libraries set out in chapter 2, there will be a premium on any approach that, like the theory of learning organizations,

- Is people centered
- Adopts an open systems approach
- Relies on the characteristics of OD
- Takes a novel view of learning in organizations

This last feature is significant, because it introduces a new element into the thinking. Modern libraries will face the managerial challenges of combining the traditional and the new, and of developing and absorbing new expertise into the organization. They will need to seek new ways of doing things, and of managing staff who will be nontraditional in terms of the library profession. They will deal with users who will take a new view of how to seek information. This will probably extend to their relationship with libraries and library staff. All this calls for a new way of looking at things, and for a different kind of learning and professional development. It will require thinking and learning in ways that challenge the accepted norms. Like all of the ideas discussed in the first two chapters of this book, there is nothing new in any of this. The idea of double-loop learning, for example, has been around since the late 1960s and early 1970s.

Double-loop learning (Bateson, 1972) is an essential part of being original. It is a tool in problem solving, it challenges conventional thinking, and it drives organizational change and OD itself. When it becomes endemic in an organization, and is systematically developed, it lays the basis of constructive and positive learning. The classical approach to management that this book argues is not adequate for today's—or more importantly tomorrow's—libraries is based on the antithesis that is single-loop learning. Single-loop organizations have a very clear differentiation between strategy and policy formulation and implementation. They rely on precedent to guide operations, and take a conventional attitude to problem solving. Their use of technology is pedestrian. They are cautious in the way that they cope with new skills requirements and with changes in the makeup, education, and training, of the workforce. They also reflect a conventional view of other related issues, like the growth in the significance of self-development.

Learning organizations, by contrast, take as one of their key principles the idea of all-pervasive learning: formal and informal, systematic, beginning with the individual, moving through and between teams, creating organizational learning. The objectives are

- To improve performance through improved skills and learning
- To use learning as a means of breaking down barriers and creating an organic, holistic organization
- To change, indeed transform, the organization
- To extend and strengthen the organizational knowledge base
- To build an organization fit for proactive change

The best books on learning organizations are still Pearn and Mulrooney (1995), and Pearn, Roderick, and Mulrooney (1995).

Knowledge Management (KM)

If the theory of learning organizations passed libraries by for the most part, the same cannot be said of Knowledge Management (KM). At least intellectually, it has been enthusiastically embraced by many managers seeking to make sense of managing in the mixed library economy of conventional and electronic information. In the survey referred to earlier, a significant majority of managers reported the practicing of knowledge management in at least some part of the organization, although its execution was usually undeveloped (Pugh, 2004). KM has also been of value for those looking to justify an enhanced role for librarians in the creation and exploitation of the intellectual capital in the organizations served by information services. In those senses, it is part of the management approach to modern libraries, and is quite clearly being successfully used today in some information sectors.

It is nevertheless still missing the point, and by some considerable distance. The first thing to be said is that however much the terminology changes, and whatever their job titles say, many librarians are more or less still doing what they have always done. Vocabularies may change, but the charge leveled at the inventors of metadata by Gorman still carries weight in this respect, and has a much wider relevance than cataloging alone:

> The idea behind metadata is that there is some Third Way of organizing and giving access in electronic resources that is approximately half way between cataloguing (expensive and effective) and keyword searching (cheap and ineffective). Further, it is alleged that such low-level bibliographic data can be supplied by authors, webmasters, publishers, and others lacking any knowledge of cataloguing.
>
> (Gorman, 2001)

This Gorman sees as "an attempt to re-invent the wheel as something other than round" (2001). Lest this appears to be Gorman pleading the case of specialization, it was emphasized earlier that he was well before his time, if not indeed a voice crying in the wilderness, in arguing for the abolition of technical services departments, using one of the theses advanced in this book—that modern library services, even at that time, called for a broad application of specialist skills in a generalist context (Gorman, 1979).

There is a vital contribution to be made by KM to the innovative management of modern library services. It has nothing to do with the impossible task of managing knowledge, because managers of knowledge we are not. Its momentous role is to do with what it says about using information as a tool to manage organizations, and using the information system as the spinal cord of the organization. KM is typically viewed as the activities and systems that go into the process of identifying, collecting, organizing, disseminating, and exploiting knowledge drawn from all the relevant sources inside and outside an organization. There is nothing new here for librarians, and the aim is one of methodically developing a comprehensive organizational knowledge base. To put it at its simplest, "The more we know, the more we are able to know" (Walters and Macrae, 2003). To this I would add that the more we know, the more we are able to know, the more responsible we will become, the more responsibility we will be able to handle, and the better our organizations will be.

KM can be used in the tasks of identifying, collecting, organizing, retrieving, disseminating, and applying all the useful information that exists in organizations. This covers information in the minds of the staff, in the results of projects, in lessons learned, in success and failure, and in planning processes. It embraces environmental monitoring, manuals, procedures, working parties, teams, and meetings. To achieve this there must be a culture that supports these activities, and a system that records and organizes the results. There must also be a coherent process of developing a structure, leadership styles, and learning systems, that all underpin this approach. This means removing obstacles to learning and communication, whether they are structural or attitudinal. KM is therefore placed fairly and squarely within the systems theory, organization development, and learning organizations orbits. Perceptive readers will have already anticipated that there is nothing new here either, but it clearly has a contemporary relevance, even if it is not as novel as its protagonists like to think.

From what has been said above, one of the key contributions of KM to organizational design is in the advancement of the technical infrastructure that is needed to do this. The nervous system of the hybrid library should be an information system that makes available

- Management information systems (MIS)
- Human resources: skills, learning, experience, interests, goals
- Administrative business: budgets, meetings, decisions
- Performance information: measures, evaluations, feedback
- Professional and technical information, issues, and developments
- Documentation from the parent organization
- The inventory
- Special projects and change initiatives
- Good practice: professional and technical
- The results of individual and group learning
- Links with other systems

(Pugh, 2001)

In hybrid libraries, the effects of this system will be significant. First, it makes for transparency. With comprehensive information systems allied to other measures, all the parts of the library are visible. It offers the possibility of dealing with the manager's major problem, that of simply knowing what is going on.

Psychologically and operationally, this is crucial because it provides the freedom, confidence, and flexibility for a change in management behavior, and the development of more relaxed and collaborative management styles. The devolution of responsibility and the empowerment of staff becomes possible in an organization that has transparency and access to information built into it as part of a system.

A sophisticated information system will also permit and sustain structural change. In this particular arena teams are important, as are associated moves away from functional to process-based organizations. These depend on the development of structures that preserve necessary specializations while applying them across internal organizational boundaries wherever they are relevant (see Gorman's point on technical services departments).

The information system will also support an organizational learning process that becomes embedded in the work of the library and the working lives of the staff. This in turn begins to deal with the major issue of multiskilling.

The change in the management ethos should embrace changes in human resource policy. Here we will look for improved access to new skills learning by making it easier for staff with new skills to move across the organization into areas where the skills can be applied.

What therefore results from a functioning information system is comprehensive organizational development affecting every area of the library and eventually creating an organization that exploits to the full the technology and the skills and abilities of the staff.

Organizations for All Seasons

As well as sharing some common ground, Systems Theory, Organization Development, Learning Organizations, and Knowledge Management hold out the hope of injecting a great deal of variety in the kind of organizations that are likely to result from the application of the ideas. They all attempt to redress the problems of the "one size fits all" approach of classical management. A focal point for this idea of differentiation can be found in Contingency Theory.

Contingency Theory

This is another idea that might have been dreamt up for hybrid libraries working in periods of uncertainty, instability and rapid change. Burns and Stalker (1961) carried out an investigation of management structures and managerial practice in 20 companies, and their work remained an influential contribution to the literature for over 30 years. One of the two basic managerial systems they identified was the organic system. This was a system working best in an unstable environment where things change rapidly and where organizational objectives will also shift in response and will of necessity be less permanent. As the advance of technology accelerates, and as societal change produces physical and digital alternatives to libraries as sources of information and alternatives to librarians as the gatekeepers of information, volatility will be an increasingly obvious characteristic of our organizational environment.

Under these conditions, organizations will thrive if they are able to change quickly themselves, realign objectives, and reorganize the way they work. Internally, there will be a less prescriptive definition of jobs and responsibilities, and networks can replace hierarchies. These networks will provide both communication and lines of authority. While specialization will still be vital, it will be more widely deployed, and it will be possible to manage different areas of the organization in different ways. Through the development of information-sharing systems, knowledge will no longer be concentrated at the top of a pyramidal organization, but will be distributed. Implicitly, this will lead to role change as managers accommodate this situation. The distinction, for example, between strategy and policy formers—the thinkers and the doers, will become less obvious.

The flexibility allowed by contingency theory has led to some criticism of it as a system that will lead to inconsistency and uncertainty as managerial practice swings between organic and bureaucratic. This tends to miss the point. No doubt it is possible to find a library at the totally bureaucratic extreme of the spectrum and another at the totally organic extreme. What it would be like to work in either of these is almost beyond imagining. In practice, most libraries will reflect a mix of management styles in any event, depending on the circumstances, the personnel involved, the degree of urgency, and the idiosyncrasies of managers. An organization can, from time to time if necessary, demonstrate mechanistic characteristics but still be rooted in the general milieu of organic organizations. Some commentators appear to assume that managerial styles can swing daily between the two poles. In fact the timescales are likely to be much longer. The ideas behind contingency theory depend on far-reaching and sustained changes. These are needed not only in structures, but in culture, management styles, leadership, communication, organizational learning and training, and job design. It is a far more pervasive system than is sometimes imagined, and it has a momentum that is hard to obstruct.

The certainty and stability that many people feel is lacking in systems like these that are strong on flexibility and weak on control comes from things like the culture. This was appropriately defined by Glass (1996) as "the way we do things around here," rather than the structure or rule book. The value of contingency theory to hybrid libraries is that it emphasizes

- Responding to, and sometimes anticipating, environmental change
- A whole-organizational dimension: Specializations can be applied across the entire working situation.
- Information systems
- Sharing knowledge
- The influence of technology as a key variable
- Integration and not separation

(Lawrence and Lorsch, 1967)

Systems theory, OD, Learning Organizations, KM, and Contingency Theory, all shed light on a different way of managing. It is a way that encourages a different form of thinking. The developmental problems of information services today call for novel solutions and new concepts. Ideas like Action Learning, Double Loop Learning, described briefly here, and other ideas like Thinking Outside the Box, convey something of the innovative nature of what we need to do. Thinking Outside the Box sums it up.

Thinking Outside the Box

One of the difficulties inherent in our present approach to managing digital libraries is that we rely too much on precedent. For guidance, we look to the things libraries did well in the past. Unfortunately, the organizational structures we used so successfully for so long are designed to work in different environments. They function best in stable operating conditions where there is a degree of certainty about what is to be done. For situations where there is uncertainty and great variety, they are not appropriate. Historical precedent alone is at least as bad for libraries as it is for any other organization. If the precedent for managing digital information is the way multimedia was managed, it is clear that there has been little thinking outside this experience, which has been misunderstood in any case. We need to learn how to examine all past experience critically and relate it to current and likely future characteristics (Nutt, 2002). Analyzing the precedents for dealing with information in different formats and challenging the assumptions on which previous practice was based are a start. Requiring proof that established ideas actually will work well, and encouraging proper debate about the premises on which libraries of the future should be organized, will lead to further progress. It could all hasten the development of more appropriate ideas on which to base the management of e-libraries.

We are responding to technological change, social change, educational change, the need for entrepreneurialism in library services, changes in user perceptions, cross-sectoral collaboration, and competition. The sum of this is a situation that is outside the previous experience of library managers, and for which no ready templates exist. The problem of designing management systems for hybrid libraries is imprecise, and there may not be a right or wrong answer. Because of the overwhelming presence of bureaucracies in practical library management, there are few precedents, but there are existing ideas we can use as pointers. The ones mentioned in this chapter are examples of theories we might care to bend to our purposes. There are also a set of circumstances that the hybrid library possesses and which will offer a clear opportunity for thinking and organizing in a different way.

Bureaucracies That Hide Distributed Organizations

The key ideas described in this chapter all have a common purpose. They represent attempts to move away from bureaucracies. Some libraries have retained the carapace of a bureaucratic structure, with conventional reporting systems and chains of command. What is actually happening beneath the surface is more interesting. Any library with more than a handful of staff, even if it is based on a single site, has a distributed organization lurking beneath the surface. Earlier in this chapter, reference was made to staff who are better educated, who may be more aware of the potential of the knowledge they possess and the information they handle, and who have greater access to training and development than before. They might increasingly come from sectors where there is a more relaxed view of organizational structures and empowerment. Cross and Parker (2004) explore the subterranean world of social networks in organizations and make the point that many organizations have distributed groups operating in a way that bears no relationship to the organizational chart. The groups they identify are based on a social network that cuts across the formal structure. They argue that it is necessary to manage these networks, and that doing so in a

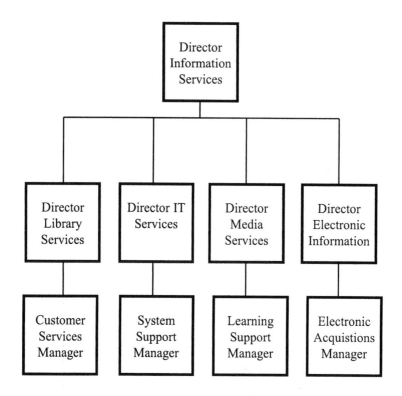

Figure 2.1 A Conventional Information Services Structure

positive way will facilitate the achievement of organizational objectives.

Fig. 2.1 is a simplification of a reasonably conventional academic information service, showing the senior staff. The structure shows clear lines of control and a clear reporting mechanism.

Within this structure, there will also be a social network, in which, for example, a system support officer reporting to the system support manager could be connected to a copyright and permissions officer reporting to the electronic acquisitions manager. The director of library services and campus library managers could be involved, as well as a media services technician reporting to the learning support manager. These people communicate across formal boundaries, and talk to each other at various levels. This social network is shown in fig. 2.2.

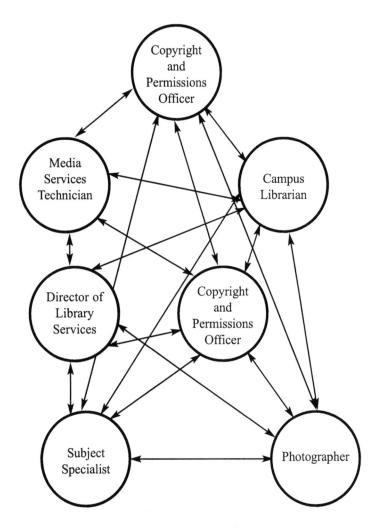

Figure 2.2 The Underlying Social Network

According to Cross and Parker (2004), this network must be analyzed and supported by managers. By undertaking network analysis, it is possible to identify key individuals in the network. These will be members of staff who are opinion formers, or who possess expertise, experience, and status that does not come from formal authority. Their influence will extend throughout the network. It will also be possible to identify individuals in the network who are under pressure, and others who have a valuable contribution to make that is underutilized. Managers who take the time to analyze these networks can improve organizational performance and achieve better use of resources and stronger communications. The networks can also serve an important motivational function and are vehicles for development, learning, and ultimately self-management. In some ways they look forward to the communities of practice of chapters 8 and 9.

It might also be possible to identify previously unknown skills and talents possessed by some staff, and that could be relevant to the work of the service.

These networks are in fact small, unrecognized, distributed organizations. The members are separated by the internal structure of the organization, yet they communicate with each other, offer support, and frequently find common cause. It is the job of the manager to:

- Identify the networks
- Identify and use the key figures—the gatekeepers to communication
- Provide support
- Incorporate the networks into the formal and informal communications systems

By doing so, a pattern of communication, influence, and collaboration can be understood in ways that cannot be discerned from looking at formal structures. This will assist managers in developing collaboration across the organization and will form a foundation for team development.

Summary

Going back to the beginning of the chapter, existing library services on the ground tend to reflect the following characteristics:

- Systematic planning
- Group working, ostensibly leading to teamwork
- Maximum throughput of standardized production
- Hierarchical management
- Activities based on formal rules
- Specialization
- Specific tasks and responsibilities for each worker
- Separation of line and staff management

- Discipline and control
- Clear lines of communication
- Clarity of management authority—only one boss in each area
- Clear boundaries within the organization
- The affirmation of management's responsibility for managing

These characteristics were ideally suited to the prevailing environment in which libraries operated. Currently, library services are beginning to reflect characteristics that are quite different from the traditional library, and within some of them there are embryo distributed organizations hard at work:

- Driven by technological change
- Specialist yet needing a broad, general application of knowledge
- Organizing combinations of print and electronic media
- Technologically complex
- Subject to complex user behavior because of the personalization of information
- Operating in unpredictable operating environments
- Subject to competition
- Already demonstrating some of the characteristics of distributed organizations, with proto-teams forming across internal boundaries

Subjecting library organizations to modern ideas about management will lead to new thinking, new ways of solving problems, and new ways of looking at how library services can be provided. This sentence is a handy definition of another idea that has been around for a very long time, and that is organizational creativity. The list of characteristics above amounts to a description of a fertile breeding ground for creativity in the organizational context.

The Conditions for Creativity in Organizations

Organizational creativity is the ideal piece of management theory for digital or electronic libraries. It depends first on bringing together opposites. The potential for e-libraries is enormous, made up as they are of

- Librarians
- Information technology specialists
- Media technologists
- Graphic designers

- Web designers
- Web masters
- Increasingly, people from other professions moving into information services

If the differences and ambiguities are allowed to flourish in an organization, they lead to what is called creative abrasion (Hirshberg, 1998). This happens when people feed off each other, show each other different perspectives, and share different ways of thinking. The result in fact is unconventional thinking, which was earlier referred to as "thinking outside the box." To get to this, organizations need

- Boundary spanning structures to put people with different characteristics into situations where they work together and produce new ideas
- The positive encouragement of friction, stemming from the juxtaposition of groups displaying differences
- Learning from others with different perspectives and from oneself

Considering changes in responsibility, in the way that jobs are delineated, and thinking about learning and increasing knowledge capital, leads into one of the key conditions on which the creative approach to management depends—that of organizational redundancy (Morgan, 1997).

Organizational Redundancy

This means give each individual, and each part of the organization, more skills than they need, more information than they need, more knowledge than they need, and more responsibility than they need to do their immediate jobs. This is part of job enrichment, job enlargement, and communication.

If we can begin to create overlaps in responsibility, we create ambiguity. Ambiguity is something which bureaucracies abhor, but a more relaxed view would suggest that ambiguity will lead to more creativity. Ownership, which is yet another principle of the bureaucracy, ought not to be a problem in electronic libraries or where there is any kind of networked information. Why should a group of staff have sole responsibility for something when others in other parts of the organization can contribute? Going back to the analogy with the catalogers, why should the group of staff holding more information about the collections than anybody else be locked away within a strict functional department? Deployed according to a very differ-

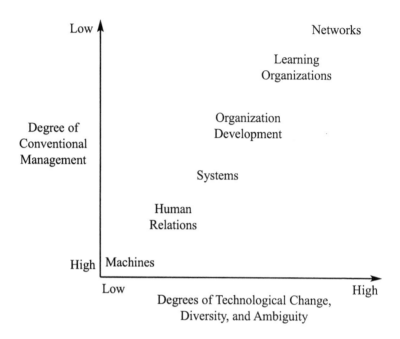

Fig. 2.3 The Relationship between Conventional Management, Change, Diversity, and Ambiguity

ent principle, their expertise could still be applied, but could be made available to users in a more direct and expansive way. Why should there be a rigid demarcation between librarians, information technologists, graphic designers, and so on? If we give a task to more than one individual or more than one team, we begin to create some multiple perspectives, and we start to harness all the available talent. Our analyses will be sharper, and our organizations better fitted to operate in the kind of environment we can expect in the e-future. If we blur the distinctions between managers and managed, between leaders and followers, between strategy and implementation, between thinkers and doers, then we can begin to accept that in the organizations of the future we should all be strategists, leaders, thinkers, doers, teachers, and learners. What we need is a theory that recognizes this, and a structure that makes it possible, so that we can make the very best use of the key talents in the e-library, which will be the staff. However this is done, we need to stop thinking about conventional principles because they lead to conventional organizational structures that are seen as fixed, concrete entities. It is time to think of libraries as organisms that duplicate and overlap each other, that have ambiguities, inconsistencies, and are untidy. It is also time to accept that this is good and creative.

Organizational Creativity: The Main Issues

We have known about creativity in organizations for over 50 years. It means the ability to think differently, to generate novel solutions to problems, and to deal with new situations that might not be susceptible to conventional thinking. It depends on people

- Learning
- Thinking
- Applying the results

Organizational creativity requires far-reaching change in the entire organizational setup and behavior. Above all, it demands structural change. Most conventional libraries can be described as "psychic prisons" (Morgan, 1997). Because they are so rigid, they restrict people's thinking. They also restrict the ability to learn by locking specialists into boxes, by dividing organizations vertically, by relying on strong control mechanisms, and by discouraging divergent thinking and risk taking. Building and sustaining organizations that will be good at changing and coping with change forced upon them depends on how creative we can be, and the first prerequisite is a permissive structure. Fig. 2.3 demonstrates the way that thinking about organizations is changing over time because of a number of influences. These ideas will form the basis for some of the structural configurations proposed in later chapters.

Chapter 3

Structures

The argument about structures—things that are often taken for granted in real life libraries—is central to the development of management practice. For most of the time, structures have been used in almost a purely defensive way, and they have been seen to some extent as one of the controlling mechanisms of the bureaucratic approach. Information services face globalization in much the same way as other enterprises, and there is no reason why our response to this cannot be characterized by an irresistible drive toward process-oriented, flatter-shaped, cross-functional organizations based on new leadership and reorganized human resource management:

> Libraries face the same change problems as most other human enterprises: the massive challenge of technology; more complex and interrelated problems [to be solved]; shorter time spans; problem-solving that has to be innovative because old solutions will not work; a need to build cross-boundary and cross-sector collaboration; a need for management styles based on identifying common interests and sharing; personnel who are willing to take responsibility for their own work and share some management responsibility; more discerning users who are also ready to exercise some control over how their needs are met; competition and the loss of a previously unchallenged position. This list does not include everything and while it is applicable to libraries it is actually taken from a global view of what is happening to business, industry, commerce, education, ecology, religion, politics, government and in the American parlance "not-for-profit" organizations.

> (Lipman-Blumen, 1996, from Pugh, 2000)

47

The Problem with Structures

An unfortunate consequence of the widespread deployment of the bureaucracy in libraries is that structures are not only seen as controlling mechanisms rather than enabling agencies, but also as insulators. One of the purposes of a traditional organizational structure is, as far as possible, to reduce organizational uncertainty. This not only works within the organizational boundaries, but also cushions the organization from environmental shocks. Any systems for monitoring boundaries in bureaucracies tend to be formal, and naturally deal with information about environmental changes by putting it through the formal communication system. This is vertical and top down, and the system is slow to react and produce results. It has within it many built-in barriers and filters; it is not really appropriate for analyzing and responding to rapid environmental change. Nor is it the case that conventional structures actually help prosecute change and development when it does take place, because of the inbuilt inertia of bureaucracies.

On the other hand, a number of writers attest that there is no hard evidence of any organizational structure being more effective than any other. In support of this position, in the United States there have been examples of very bureaucratic organizations with an impressive record of innovation. During the late 1980s and early 1990s, *Fortune 500* regularly awarded prizes for innovation to at least one large, highly centralized, almost autocratic organization that produced stunning commercial results.

To confuse the matter further, at the other end of the scale it is also true that in general the most adaptable organizations may be those Mintzberg (1979) termed primitive: possessing total flexibility, able to change direction quickly, multiskilled and with generic job descriptions, if these existed at all, because of the small number of people involved. They also had permeable internal boundaries with a fuzzy and imprecise division of labor. The result was organizations that were highly attuned to environmental disturbance. This could almost be a recipe for managing 21st century libraries, and what has tipped the balance in favor of this kind of structure is the overall implication of the changes referred to in the first two chapters. Users are now showing signs of developing an integrated approach to meeting their own information needs. One day this will involve them in using the "seamless web" of information provision, dotted throughout the theory of library management, for themselves, without the aid of a librarian. Lankes and others (2003), arguing from an American perspective, states that "the use of freely available web-based resources are roughly equivalent to the use of other resources." Others might wish to take issue with this, but it is an identifiable trend, and libraries need to be organized in ways that reflect it. They also need to be organized in ways that make the best use of this hybridization. This is where structures come in. In particular, they will influence the application of skills. "Narrow expertise in a single area . . . is no longer sufficient" (Brickley et al, 2003) but there is no point in developing broad expertise if it is confined by structures. An overwhelming majority of library managers consulted in the previously mentioned survey (Pugh, 2004) indicated that it would be difficult for staff who mastered new skills to move into an area of the library where they could be used.

In future library organizations will have distributed decision-making centers. Their communication systems will be diffuse. Structures will be flatter. There will have to be a culture of learning, collaboration, and teamwork. Multiple leadership that is motivational, participative, and supportive will aid this, and it will be a new form of leadership. Decision making will be decentralized. Organizations in general will exhibit a flexibility that allows skills to be acquired, that fosters professional and personal development, and allows talent to be applied wherever it is relevant. All in all, the result will be a healthier, but more provocative, working environment. Hopefully it will also be run by provocative and questioning staff who thrive in this environment. All of these features depend on structural change.

Libraries will certainly be populated by provocative and questioning users, some of whom have always been like this. The difference is that they are growing more confident and certain of their rights, and we will be dealing with a different user approach. Information seekers will be more adept and increasingly sure of their own ability to navigate the information landscape. Compared with the static, prescriptive way in which libraries traditionally met user needs, the demands made will be unpredictable, catholic, and inclusive.

It will not stop with the clientele. We can expect to see alliances and networks between information providers grow significantly. This will increasingly bring together services with different traditions, priorities, and objectives. Collaboration will call for the ability to negotiate and share, and as these networks of collaborating information providers expand, they will not be amenable to the familiar command and control mechanisms of conventional management.

The first step in developing a management style and system that is appropriate for the 21st century is to change the way we look at structures. Chapter 2, in considering the potential contribution of network analysis to library development, exposed one of the weaknesses of the current approach to structures. The tendency is to consider structures from a formal standpoint, mainly as representations of the distribution of authority and the location of power within an organization. They are also regarded as the depiction of reporting mechanisms and vertical communication channels. The natural reaction to a request to describe any organization is to draw the organizational hierarchy starting from the top, with a box labeled director, and working downwards. This is fine as far as it goes, and it can tell the observer a lot about the organization, but it is incomplete. One way to counteract this is to develop a new way of conceptualizing organizations.

How to Look at Structures

Brickley and others (2003) make use of the term "organizational architecture" to describe a phenomenon that covers culture and decision making among other things. It supports the exercise of authority, provides information, and facilitates empowerment, motivation, and leadership. Allee (2003) makes the point that the

> organizational chart is yielding to maps of network relationships across the company. Organizational models include external participation as well as those who are direct employees. . . . An equally important network pattern to trace is the way knowledge networks and communities of practice help generate and spread knowledge. Knowledge sharing tends to follow the lines of social interactions, so it is important to understand how interactions are helping or hindering the diffusion of innovation across the organization.

This is a key issue for bureaucracies. It is much more difficult for networking and the spread of knowledge to take place when there are internal barriers. These can take the form of specialization, standardization, and vertical communication that has to penetrate a number of organizational layers to get to the people that are at the library-user interface. Rigid structures are the most obvious internal barriers in the organization. Apart from blocking communication and knowledge sharing, it is also more difficult to develop an appropriate leadership style. This is the kind of leadership that relies less on formal authority and charisma and more on the softer skills of facilitating, motivating, coaching, and creating a working situation that allows people to apply their skills and express their abilities to the full.

Developing a new approach to organizations depends on jettisoning conventional thinking and seeing structure as a mix of how people behave, how they relate to others both professionally and personally, how they communicate, and what they believe in, as well as organizational forms. It also means seeing the link between structure and a number of other things. It is

connected with the way the organization handles its learning, or, if preferred, develops its intelligence. It influences the identification and management of the knowledge and information accrued by individuals and
groups, and supports the growth of this knowledge base. Last but not least,
thinking about appropriate structures means taking into account, as a key
aspect of organizational life, the social networks described in chapter 2 and
in chapters 8 and 9.

This widens consideration of structure, so that it includes

- The learning system—individual learning, group learning, learning from
  work, self-learning
- The technological infrastructure
- The social network
- The activities of formal and informal groups or teams

All of these factors impinge on how decisions are taken, strategies evolved,
and policies formulated. Their influence on how day-to-day operations are
executed and overseen is powerful. They have implications for management attitudes, styles, and behavior.

Allee (2003), in her pivotal discussion of organizations as living systems, identifies three key elements in the consideration of structure:

- The pattern of an organization, meaning the relationships between the
  key components of the system
- The structure, which is best seen simply as a physical presentation of
  the formal relationships referred to above
- The activity, which is what actually goes on in an organization. This
  includes the informal networks referred to here and in other chapters.

Perhaps the key issue in considering the structure in this way is its relationship with change. If there is to be any significant change in organizations, then it will have to be something that comes from within. While it
may well be triggered by an issue in the organizational environment, the
change itself will be an internal process. As such it will depend on decisions
taken by the organizational players, and will reflect attitudes, beliefs, and
personalities. It has been said elsewhere that the biggest single factor influencing the way an organization is managed is the personality of the manager—that, and the structure, which is in some ways the product of the
manager's personality.

The reform of a library to make it fit for the 21st century involves a
number of overlapping and interlocking initiatives. At bottom it is about

developing the capacities of the people who make the organization work. This requires the creation and sharing of knowledge about the organization, its users, and the environment in which it exists. It requires systematic communication through formal and informal channels, and it depends on the growth of a strong culture that reflects how people feel about the library, and how they behave inside the organization. It is a collaborative task, and it touches on much more than the mere shape an organization takes.

Summary: Why Are Structures Important?

Some managers would say they are not, particularly in the developing context of the digital library and distributed collections, where technology will ensure there will be no barriers, and will bring about fluidity and flexibility. On the contrary, if structures are viewed in the light of Allee's three elements and the comments earlier, they are a key feature and have a number of key purposes. It is also helpful to view the three elements above as essentially interlinked. Structures are indicators of several characteristics.

Managerial Attitudes

Structures are devised by managers who, whatever pressures come from other forces, actually make the decisions on the form their libraries will take. Structures are usually dictated by the managerial assessment of what is needed to run a particular organization, and the resulting shape has a critical influence on how everything else in the organization operates. These decisions on structures will be influenced by a number of factors:

- An assessment of the environment
- The preferred managerial style. This includes
  - How decisions are taken
  - How communication is managed
  - The attitude to learning
- A view of the abilities, attitudes, and behaviors of the personnel
- The influence of the parent organization
- The generally accepted way of managing within the sector
- The organizational culture

Colored by these and other influences, it is usually a manager, sometimes in discussion with others, who decides what form an organization will take. In designing libraries for the e-future, the place to start is then with managerial behavior, because this is often harder to change than anything else, everything else depends on it, and the formal structure is a virtually infallible indicator of what this behavior will be. It is asking a great deal to expect managers, or anybody else in the organization, to change behaviors and embrace the subtle traits of coaching, facilitating learning, acting as mentors, and learning new leadership behaviors. Without removing the structural impediments, and putting in place an enabling structure, it is also futile.

Instruments of Change

Beginning this section with a question—can bureaucracies support teams?—will illustrate the significance of structure as a change agent. From time to time in professional writing there are minor eruptions around this theme. The answer is no, provided that there is a clear understanding of what constitutes a real team (see chapters 8 and 9). Any kind of organizational development in the digital world will require a structure that supports team development rather than inhibits it. Teams, likely to be at the heart of library design for the future, are a piece of major structural change. Roles, internal dynamics, skills, leadership, and communication are rightly given much weight, but without the structural change on which teams must be based, they will not work. So the structure is not only the first indicator of the managerial approach. In the process of organization development and behavior change, it is the first thing to alter.

Facilitators of Learning

Learning will be at the heart of new organizations. The kind of learning that will be needed will

- Challenge existing thinking
- Help in the development of new ways of thinking
- Make a dynamic contribution to problem solving
- Support organizational development
- Increase and extend the skills base

There is no benefit in any of these things if they continue to be circumscribed by a staid and stuffy monolithic structure. They need a support mechanism that offers a framework for behavior while still encouraging the organizationwide application of skills and knowledge.

Learning has always gone on in organizations, but until relatively recently it has been mainly viewed as an individual responsibility, and considered as something that might help the individual to do a better job. Learning in modern organizations is more potent if it is seen as a collective issue, based more on collaboration in the workplace, with a broader perspective, and with a fix on the organization rather than the individual. Any kind of structure that has strong and inbuilt specialization, clear task and role boundaries, and is disposed to eliminate ambiguity and work with certainties, will not encourage new learning. This can only come from the elimination of internal boundaries, whether they are hierarchical and power based, or tied to roles and functions.

Frameworks for Communication

Like conventional learning in organizations, communication in bureaucracies runs along the structural fault lines, and is subject to the same strictures. Structure is crucial in sustaining communication, but like learning it has to flow across the organization.

What Are the Possibilities?

What we are looking for can be summed up by returning to Allee (2003): a view of the organization as a living system, founded on the feature that forms all living systems—the network. The options for organizations are a structure that is closed, as in a bureaucracy, or open, with greater receptiveness to the environment and powerful internal openness, as in more organic organizational forms.

Organization development in librarianship starts from a rigid, mechanistic position. Organizations have been based on ensuring predictability, maintaining control, and eliminating complexity. Control was exercised from the top layer of the pyramid, and specialization and the breaking down of the organization into segments were the norms. As thinking changed, the concept of the organization moved away from that of the machine bureaucracy. At different times, our reference points for how we organize work have been political systems, cultural systems, open systems, biological systems, networks, and all of these together.

There is a development in the thinking about organizational forms, from the rigidity of the classical and scientific school to the more flexible forms implied by the views of organizations as open systems or as networks.

Biological theories of change—that is the idea of the organizational life cycle—have also been advanced, and the idea of the living network has emerged from some of the ideas described in chapter 2. Most obviously, the living networks concept takes in some aspects of system theory, plus a view of network analysis. It also builds on characteristics of the organization design approach, learning organizations, and knowledge management. Latterly, a preoccupation with creativity, ambiguity, and organizational redundancy has emerged. All of these come together in the idea of organizations as living systems.

The Organization as Brain

Morgan (1997) saw a developing trend from the view of the organization as machine through the image of it as a network to the motif of the organization as brain. Although the view of the brain sometimes put forward by management theorists has been debunked by serious neurologists (Rose, 2005), Morgan's views are a useful reference point for taking things a little further and are a graphic representation of the idea of a living network. In the context of today's hybrid library they are particularly attractive. The following is a summary of Morgan's views. Organizations should be

- Distributed so that in the event of a catastrophe, any part can take over the functions of another. It was conventionally thought that the brain's right hemisphere controlled intuitive thinking, while the left was the center of rationality. It is now believed that the relationship between the hemispheres is more complex, and that they can in fact replace each other and duplicate each other's functions.
- It follows that there is no single center of power or control.
- Each part of the organization could act independently if necessary.
- Each is also part of the greater whole. It uses the information system and possesses all of the information, characteristics, and skills of the whole organization.
- At the same time, each part is capable of replacing the entire organization if it is necessary.

What is written above is a massive oversimplification, and I would suggest that interested readers should look at Rose (2005). Nevertheless the characteristics outlined are useful and are related to organizational redundancy—another relevant concept.

Organizational Redundancy

- 90 percent of the brain can be removed and it will still continue to operate, according to Morgan.

- The same could apply to the organization's essential systems.

There are well-documented accounts of medical patients who, having suffered massive trauma leading to a complete loss of the power of speech, have made full recoveries and learned to speak again by being trained to use a different part of the brain. In other words, it could be beneficial to create an organization where the parts have more power than they need for their normal functions and can duplicate the activity of other parts. Some of the organization is potentially redundant because of this.

Organizational redundancy is a critical contribution to breaking down internal boundaries. It is a way of creating overlapping roles and responsibilities: give each individual and each part of the organization

- More skills than they need
- More information than they need
- More knowledge than they need
- More responsibility than they need

to do their immediate jobs. This will help to create some ambiguity, where traditional organizations by contrast emphasize clarity. The trick is to blur the distinctions between

- Managers and managed
- Leaders and followers
- Strategy and implementation
- Thinkers and doers

Informed managers could then take things a little further and give a project to two project teams. What sort of creativity will come from this? What sort of novel solutions will come from attacking a problem from more than one angle?

Tackling structure in this way has a number of effects:

- It creates the abrasion vital to organizational creativity. The ability to think differently and to solve problems in novel ways is critical in modern organizations. So is the skill of dealing with situations that are themselves novel and might not be susceptible to conventional thinking. Both of these gain from the contributions of people coming from different perspectives. It depends on making use of the fuzziness and ambiguity created by the lack of clarity about where responsibilities begin and end. Maximizing this can create situations where people learn from each other by tackling the same issues from different standpoints and applying the results.

- Decision making, strategy formulation, and objective setting also improve.
- The network at the heart of the living organization is then shaped by the overlaps and dual responsibilities, uncertainties about roles, tasks, and internal section boundaries.
- The organization begins to reflect the workings of the social network which is described in chapter 2.

These principles involve change in all parts of the organization, and this underscores the point that structures are not merely ways of describing the physical shape of an organization. They say something about the philosophy and the culture as well. Following these ideas through will involve job enrichment, job enlargement, and different patterns of communication. If we can begin to create overlaps in responsibility, we create ambiguity. This is something which bureaucracies abhor, but a more thoughtful view would suggest that ambiguity will lead to more creativity.

Weakening internal boundaries and developing overlapping areas of influence will strike at a particularly invidious characteristic of bureaucracy, which is the idea of ownership. When the assumption takes hold that a particular section of an organization has proprietary rights over something, it can make communication and collaboration even more difficult. The diffuse nature of electronic information, networked information, or e-libraries should mean that we can develop a more nuanced view of this issue. Ownership then becomes a collective matter, as indeed does responsibility.

The critical response to these ideas about responsibility and ownership is to say that they will lead to chaos and a paralyzed organization that will underachieve. The point is that collective responsibility will still reside with teams or other groups, and ultimate responsibility will remain with managers, although they will behave in different ways. The overlaps and uncertainties, coupled with the development of networks, will lead to a cultural change. It will become accepted that other people, with no direct involvement in a particular issue but with a valid opinion or information, can make an input. Specialization and vertical divisions always lead to territorial claims and prevent the free exchange of ideas. Why should a group of staff have sole responsibility for something when others in other parts of the organization can contribute? Why should there be a rigid demarcation between librarians, information technologists, graphic designers, and so on? If we give a task to more than one individual, or more than one team, we begin to create some multiple perspectives. We also contribute to the emergence of super teams, as contributions from members of other teams are encouraged. When we start to harness all the available talent, our analyses will be sharper and our organizations better fitted to operate in the kind of environment we can expect in the e-future. If we can make it harder to discern differences between managers and managed, between leaders and followers, between strategy and implementation, between thinkers and doers, then we can begin to accept that in the organizations of the future we should all be all of these things, and teachers and learners as well.

What we need is a structure that recognizes all this and makes these things possible so that we can make the very best use of the key talents in the e-library, which will be the staff. However this is done, we need to stop thinking about organizational structures as fixed, concrete entities. It is time to think of them as being made up of organisms that duplicate and overlap each other, that have ambiguities, inconsistencies, and are untidy. It is also time to accept that this is good and creative. Brickley and others (2003) used the example of the jazz quartet:

- They decide which song they will play.
- They have an agreed view of the orchestration in general.
- They each agree which instruments they will play.
- They work together.

All this ensures that there is some functionality and some sense of responsibility, but there are other more interesting results:

- They do not all necessarily play the same tune.
- The result of the interaction of these functions is the process—the delivery of the music to the listener.

If we can visualize an organization that works like this, we are envisioning something in which there is both specialization and all-round skills. It is an organization in which each part is linked to the others so that there is a free flow of information around and across the entire organization. It is a situation in which each part has the skills, power, and resources to take over the work of another part, and in which each part operates as a microcosm of the whole. We will then be getting close to what is needed for the e-future. Paradoxically, we are also getting close to reinventing Mintzberg's primitive organization, which in some ways is the best equipped to deal with the e-future. This is small, adaptable, quick to change direction, and operates with a minimum of rules. It is made up of multiskilled specialists who fill whatever roles the circumstances require. It often has more than one leader, and has no separation of strategy, policy, or implementation. It is almost the epitome of the team-based organization referred to earlier. Structurally, it is also a good example of Allee's living network.

Living Networks

"The pattern of organization in a living system is that of an autopoietic network" (Allee, 2003). The language surrounding this theory is, like metadata, extremely dense, and the simplest way of applying the idea to organizations is to say that an autopoietic organization is no more and no less than a living organization. It is capable of change, of regeneration, and of development. It responds to conditions in its environment, but does it in a way that marks it out from the mechanistic organizations that have been typical of libraries throughout their history. A bureaucracy does not really respond to changes and threats in its environment. Constrained by its structure, it tries to minimize the threats and disturbances. The living system is based on a network, and this network can include other networks outside the organization, such as communities of users and other information services, sometimes operating in other sectors of the profession. It will increasingly include commercial providers of information. A library created in this way is essentially different from a bureaucracy, first of all in the nature of its components. Here we can go back to the earlier metaphors of the organization as brain, and the organization as jazz band. In both organisms

- Power is distributed.
- There is no single center.
- All are capable of both independent action and close collaboration.
- There is an overall concept.
- The organism is capable of reproducing itself, thus it can create suborganisms that duplicate the parent. This is similar to Morgan's depiction of the organization as brain.
- What is delivered is a process, not a function.

This last point represents an important distinction. Many libraries are functionally organized in that they are broken down into sections, departments, or divisions that each deliver a discrete aspect of the service to users. A process-based organization is set up as units that manage the entire process of the delivery of information to a group of users, from the identification of information through its organization to its exploitation. This is arguably a more intelligible process to the user, and a more logical way of ensuring that all the talents and knowledge of library staff are applied wherever relevant. The vital argument here is that it is this same process-based approach that is being followed by the expert electronic information user who is increasingly adept at identifying multimedia sources, collecting data, delivering it to the desktop, and storing and using it.

What this means is that living organizations, whether using the brain metaphor or the jazz band metaphor, are different from the bureaucracy. They are distinctive in terms of their culture, the way that the parts combine, their internal and external relationships, and their social processes.

This leads to another primary characteristic of the living organization, and that is the place in it that is occupied by organizational learning. The creation of knowledge is a crucial function and comes from the interaction of individuals and the parts of the organization, and from the organization's links with its environment.

Also crucial is how this knowledge is preserved, processed, and shared for the benefit of the organization. These purposes are served by the structure of the organization and by the communication system. In a bureaucracy, the communication of anything formal will first follow the pattern of interaction imposed by the structure: Knowledge will flow up and down, and to a lesser extent across. With a little luck, it will also follow the pattern dictated by the social network. By contrast, the living organization is *all* network. All forms of individual and group learning and information transfer are embraced by the network, across and throughout the organization. So the social network is formalized. The information system also ensures that the organization retains the knowledge that it acquires. Knowledge creation and dissemination are therefore overt functions of the living organization, and form part of the central core.

The emergence of the electronic library has refocused attention on an organizational dilemma. This is the issue of specialization versus integration. Usually resolved by conventional management in favor of specialization, it has been given added piquancy by the implications of some of the theories discussed earlier: organizational creativity, the importance of creative friction, and the concept of the "seamless web of information," among others. Topics like the balance between control and empowerment have a fresh significance. The tension between clearly defined roles and responsibilities and the cross-boundary and cross-sectoral working indicated by emerging trends in information provision is another issue. So are the huge questions of the organizational information system and organizational learning.

The Options

Perhaps it should be repeated here that there is no evidence that a bureaucracy will not work in delivering modern information services and that there is so far no empirical evidence that it will not be the most efficient way of doing so. Nevertheless, the argument is still that there will be better ways of capitalizing on the opportunities for organizational development offered by the mixed environment. As far back as 1973, Child pointed out that approaches based on regulation, little differentiation, functional hierarchy, specialization, and expertise were not good where there is a high degree of uncertainty and change.

I am almost sure that Child would also have pointed out today that the organization described here is a better way of making use of the burgeoning skills of technologists. At the same time, this organization will reaffirm the value of the traditional skills, and release creative energy, by developing dynamic partnerships between differing professions and traditions. There are a number of options for implementing organizational forms that are more appropriate to contemporary and coming circumstances.

Process-Based Structures

The process that libraries are engaged in is the delivery of information to users. This process includes a number of functions, and these revolve around the identification, acquisition, organization, access to, and delivery of both conventionally packaged information and digital information. The information can be held in-house and on networks where the content is owned by other providers. The users can be remote or physically adjacent. Sometimes a proportion of the staff can also be remote.

All of the functions described rely on a degree of specialized knowledge, training, and skills. Yet many of the skills, and certainly much of the knowledge, will also be applicable across the spectrum of user needs, and can represent a contribution way outside a narrow specialization. The trick is to organize the process in a way that maintains the specialization while allowing the expertise to be applied across the board.

Matrix Structures

Matrix structures focus on groups of specialists who are brought into a multidisciplinary or a multifunctional team that is working on a project. Simultaneously, they retain their day-to-day responsibility, reporting, and control mechanisms. In some cases they can be permanent organizational features or they can be project-based units. Matrix structures are felt to be particularly effective in situations where things are changing quickly. They are also seen to be useful where there is a degree of discretion about how to work, and where specialist expertise has to be applied to problem solving or developmental issues. They may now be less fashionable in libraries than they were, although there is some evidence (Pugh, 2004) that they are still enticing prospects for some library managers.

Teams

The structure that brings together the best features of the process-based approach and the matrix, and to a considerable degree ameliorates the difficulties, is the team structure (see chapters 8, 9, 10). The focal point of the teams could be services to groups of users distinguished by subject, by geographical location, market segment, or mode of study, but not specialized forms of material. Used in this way, teams rehabilitate what was earlier described as perhaps the best way of organizing hybrid libraries —Mintzberg's primitive organization. This was characterized by

- Flexibility
- Adaptability
- Multiskilling
- Differentiation
- Use of specialization
- Shared leadership
- Shared strategy and policy formulation
- Sensitivity to environmental change
- An emphasis on learning
- The creative use of differences
- Powerful lateral communications

The link between some of the characteristics and organizational creativity will not be missed. There are obvious possibilities for overlapping responsibilities in the connections between teams, and the membership of more than one team. Exposure to differences is encouraged because teams bring together personnel from different professional backgrounds. They should also encourage multiple leadership. The construct is a step towards the living organization, in that teams themselves are networks. They also network with other teams and develop multiple channels of communication.

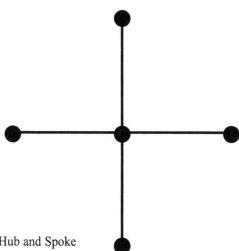

Fig. 3.1 The Hub and Spoke

Systems-Based Structures

These are a more expansive development, including elements of both the process and the matrix structures. As most system-based structures will be team-based, they also support broader relationships across the entire organization and outside the organizational boundaries.

To put the finishing touches to this conception of organizations, it is necessary to take a multilayered, or multidimensional, view. The organization, while it is flatter, still has a structure. Superimposed on this is an information system that acts as the neural cortex. The argument is for a concept of the organization that is more than a concentration on the shape, on the number of layers, and on the traditional allocation of roles and descriptions of jobs. In this case, the information system and the way knowledge is disseminated call for some attention.

Communication

In this chapter much has been made of the problems of effective communication in organizations with traditional structures. The capacity of the hierarchical system to distort and limit communication as it passes through the organizational levels is well known. The informal communication system that grows up in all organizations, but is probably more prevalent in bureaucracies, also leads to problems. Informal communication systems often give the participants the chance to exercise some choice over whom

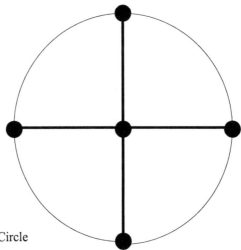

Fig. 3.2 The Circle

they talk to. People have a tendency to talk to recipients they think share their views, or with whom they have interests in common, and they might also talk only to people whom they consider to be of the same status as themselves. Sometimes they will talk to people outside their part of the official network but whom they think will offer political advantages. In this way, the emergence of informal gatekeepers, players who decide who else will participate in the communication, are widespread. In formal communication systems gatekeepers exist by virtue of their position in the hierarchy. Here there is an inevitable tendency to filter the sorts of messages that are circulated. This is most often seen in the roles of middle management.

It was suggested earlier that bureaucracies are designed to produce conformity: This is equally true of their communication systems. The result is that the new perspectives that are essential for organizational growth are unlikely to be freely and widely aired. Unless communication is treated as a subsystem of the organization, these behavioral phenomena are equally unlikely to occur as far as communication in organic structures is concerned. Also, where there is organizational complexity, and particularly if there are uncertainties in the environment, there is an added strain on communication patterns. It should be noted here (see chapters 8 and 9) that teams can also impede communication. This is particularly true when group think begins to emerge.

The solution is of course the amalgamation of formal and informal communication systems into one. As we are eliminating the communication patterns of the bureaucracy, with its vertical lines and limited horizontal interface, we are left with three options.

The Hub and Spoke

Fig. 3.1 shows this form, typically adopted by libraries with strong bureaucratic tendencies and multiple service points. Communication was between the units on the periphery and the center. It had the potential for overwhelming centralization, and the communication system was in practice as inflexible and incomplete as the bureaucracy that supported it.

The Circle

In this structure, the units along the boundary communicate with each other and the hub, as shown in fig. 3.2. A definite improvement on the hub and spoke, it still manifested many of the problems found in the sort of organizations that tend towards overcentralization.

Networks

Fig. 3.3 shows the living network. The social, operational, and managerial units are the teams. The network is formed on one level by the links between individual team members, by overlapping responsibilities, and by elements of common membership. On another level, the information system, the informal communication system, the organizational learning system, and the technological infrastructure provide the framework for communication and management.

Networks reduce the impact of the problems identified in the other structures. They are basically systems that allow every part of the organization to talk to every other part. Their key characteristics are that

- The power of the gatekeepers is reduced if not completely eliminated.
- Management control of communication is reduced.
- Openness to new ideas is encouraged.
- There is a better chance that all parts of the organization can see the whole.
- They provide a basis for supporting the kind of organization that dispenses with the ring-fencing of expertise.

Networks combine the key ideas of this chapter. They are characterizations of Morgan's parallel with the brain (1997) and Allee's exposition of living networks (2003).

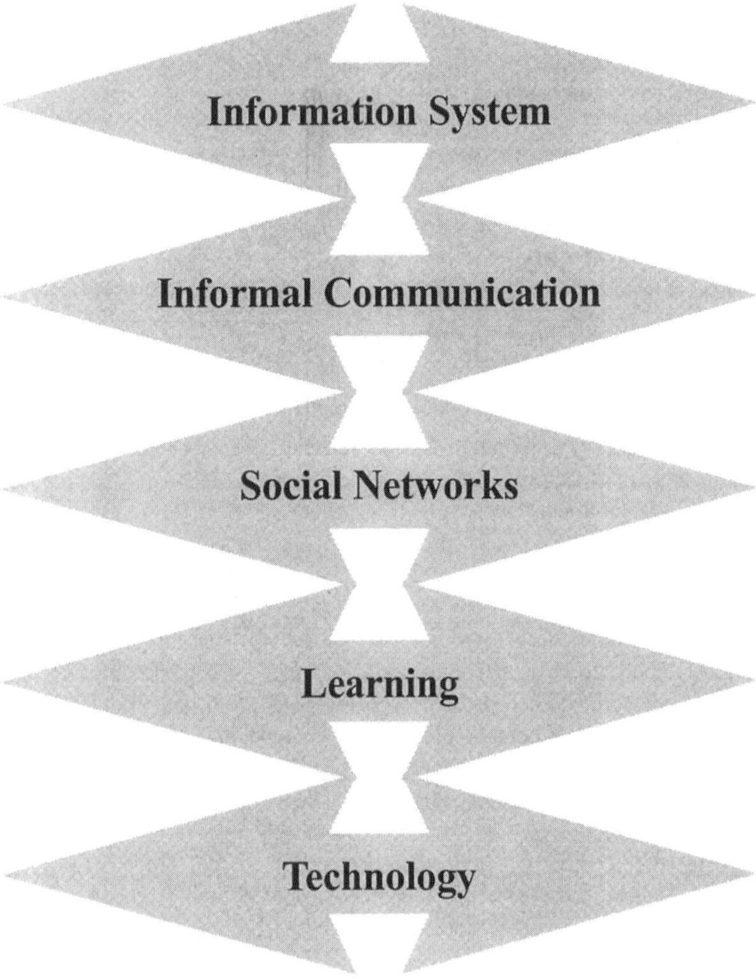

Fig. 3.3 The Living Network

A key element, that of communication between the individuals in the team and with the other teams, will follow the pattern described earlier in the chapter. It will not be based on hierarchies and reporting mechanisms, but will reflect common interests, shared specializations, shared responsibilities, shared experiences, social patterns, and sometimes multiple team membership.

The other key element in this is the social network, or the face-to-face communication between individuals in different teams. This is of crucial importance in organizations that rely in part on collaboration with other organizations or with parts of the same organization working in geographically separate locations. It is particularly relevant to a developing phenomenon that is euphemistically and inaccurately labeled the virtual team, and some of the research into this aspect is summarized in the next chapter.

As well as providing the basic social structure of the organization, the teams also represent communities of interests. The information flow between the teams is therefore made up of

- All of the knowledge networks that exist in the organization: the codified knowledge accruing from organizational activities; the personal knowledge acquired and held by individuals and groups; knowledge held by personnel systems—knowledge held in the formal system.
- The implicit knowledge, often part of the history of the organization: the informal accounts of how things were done; of the actions of individuals; of the way that key players acted; stories that are told—in sum, part of the culture.
- The informal knowledge that is created, uncovered, and communicated as part of the social process of work and communication.

(Allee, 2003)

The sources of this knowledge will be in the life of the organization: meetings, projects, operations, strategy and policy formulation, and learning. This underlines the argument for the adoption of organic structures and for looking at structures from the systems point of view. Only a fluid organization can support the spread of this knowledge. The structure is then formed by

- The formal communication system
- The informal communication system on a social level
- The learning system
- The technology used: to create the network, to make links, to "find and disseminate information" (Allee, 2003), to manage the content, to help apply the knowledge and learning to the needs of the organization.

The missing element in this is the accompanying behavior change by managers and managed. This issue will be examined later. For now, it is sufficient to note the characteristics of the kind of organizations that might emerge and mark them down as having a key influence on the skills issue, to be discussed in the next chapter. Organizations based on living networks, although they exist in theory more than in practice, are said to be

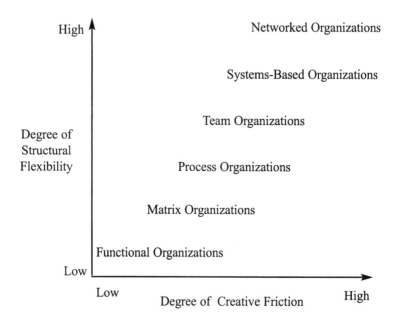

Figure 3.4 Structural Flexibility and Creative Friction

- Environmentally sensitive—possessed of the skills of learning, and changing in step with the changes in their operating environments
- Decentralized
- Reflecting dispersed power centers and multiple decision making
- Committed to individual development

(De Geus 2002)

Fig. 3.4 shows the relationship between creative abrasion or friction in organizations and changes in organizational forms. The case study which follows is based on an actual situation that was faced by a library serving a major educational institution in a large metropolitan area where there was some scope for the development of the kind of initiatives referred to earlier in this text: collaborative projects that span organizational boundaries and require the participation of more than one sector within organizations—an ideal situation for developing structures and attitudes that supported creativity.

Case Study 1
MANAGING THE DISTRIBUTED
ORGANIZATION WITHOUT
STRUCTURES, WITHOUT RULES

The Situation

In the early days of automated library services, Alpha, which was a provincial university with a progressive attitude to collaboration with neighboring institutions, was anxiously seeking improvements in its services to users. Facing financial restrictions, it made some tentative moves to open discussions with another university whose campus was only a mile or two away. The intention was to develop resource sharing for the benefit of the staff and students of both institutions. Regrettably, they were rebuffed by the director of library services of the latter, with a sneering reference to "attempts to establish an egalitarian library service."

Undeterred, the director of library services began to consider the position of other educational institutions in the same city. These were a specialist college with a national reputation for the provision of courses in performing arts, and two other lower-level institutions with strong reputations in the education of engineers, paramedical disciplines, and professionals at all levels in the hospitality and tourism areas. All of these study areas were in fact common elements in all four institutions, and Alpha was already running a comprehensive staff development program that had been made available on a fee-paying basis to the other colleges. This was well patronized.

Alpha University was one of the earliest implementers of automated library systems, which at the time were beyond the resources of the other three colleges. Preliminary discussions with the other librarians indicated a major interest in the possibility of sharing access to the university's automated library management system. Following more detailed discussions, the director of library services at Alpha drew up a proposal for a cooperative network providing for the sharing of automated library facilities between the university, the two further education colleges, and the specialist college for the performing arts.

Alpha's Commitment

The information service at Alpha University undertook to provide

- Full access to a networked library management system covering the university campus and the five campuses of the partner institutions. This would include unfettered use of
    - the ordering and acquisitions system
    - the cataloguing system
    - multimedia cataloguing and lending
    - equipment loans
    - inventories
    - financial systems
- All necessary support, training, and development
- Hardware and software maintenance

These facilities and services would be available on payment of an annual fee to Alpha. Alpha agreed to give 18 months notice of an intention to dissolve the service, and the parpticipating institutions agreed to give 18 months notice of their intention to withdraw from the cooperative.

The Partners' Commitment

The other three institutions jointly agreed to

- Harmonize their cataloguing practices with those of Alpha
- Operate a common library registration policy and procedure, and use a single user card that would allow access to all the library service points in the cooperative
- Continue to work together on the development of collaborative and mutually beneficial projects
- Run the project as a collaborative undertaking with each chief librarian in turn acting as a coordinator for an agreed period

The terms of the agreement were enshrined in a letter of intent agreed to by all four partners. This letter also set out a number of principles that all parties agreed were crucial to the success of the partnership.

Equality

Although one institution was clearly considerably bigger than the other three and had undertaken the lion's share of the project development, it was unanimously agreed that there would be no senior partner. The rotation of responsibility for coordination was a strong element in this. It was also agreed that any one of the partners could ask for a meeting to be convened to discuss any issue arising from the collaboration at any time. On the part of the current convener, there was an obligation to call the meeting.

Contributions to the running costs of the project would also be on an equal basis, and there would be no limitations imposed on the shared use of facilities.

Mutuality

All parties to the agreement accepted the crucial nature of the relationships and the equality of the arrangements. They each acknowledged the common benefits to be derived from working together. It was clearly perceived that interdependence was a way of raising quality for everyone. There was also an acceptance of the fact that there were many complimentary elements which could be used to the advantage of the partners.

Cross-Boundary Devices

It was accepted that the easiest form of integration—at management level—was not enough to create the maximum advantage across the board. There would therefore be a coordinated program of integrating activities for staff at all levels. This would be driven forward by the staff development program already in place, which would now place greater significance on group work and the skills of dialog and collaboration.

Communication

A communications protocol was implemented to cover

- The communication channels to be used in varying circumstances
- The procedures to be followed
- A communications timetable
- A set of rules for responding to communications, for ensuring that everybody remained in the loop, and for dealing with the social aspects

of communication
- A system for managing virtual meetings

The Result

The consortium ran for a period of almost eight years, which was a long time in the life of all the institutions involved. During those eight years, there were various college mergers, changes in the nature of the institutions and their libraries, and other innovations which meant that ultimately the system came to a natural end. One of the institutions involved merged with a much larger institution. The others eventually developed their own free-standing systems while still maintaining a high level of collaboration. The main features of this collaboration had evolved during the years of the shared facilities until they amounted to comprehensive shared services for users.

The difficulties encountered were generally reckoned to be minor—mainly related to infringements of regulations concerning the borrowing and return of material. The early agreement that any infringements would be treated as if they were infringements of regulations in the library to which the culprit formally belonged, served to deflect any possible political fallout as well as producing a speedy resolution. At a dinner looking back on the eight years of cooperation and celebrating it, there was a general view that the success of the venture could be attributed to

- The absence of a bureaucratic system of control. While this would be seen as a danger by many, to the participants it represented a flexibility which preserved the key purposes of the arrangement without introducing an administrative burden.
- Paradoxically, the existence of a communications framework. Rather than being considered as a restrictive force, this was seen as safeguarding the equality of the operation by ensuring that all communications were dealt with on the same basis and within an agreed timescale. Responses were compulsory, so nobody failed to express an opinion and take part in decision making. There was also an essential social component to electronic communication between people who were set apart not only by geographical separation but by institutional differences.
- The transfer of key knowledge and skills. As the collaboration developed, small nonhierarchical working parties were established to consider various developmental aspects. Running alongside the thriving

staff development program managed by Alpha, which in addition exposed staff to influences from outside the consortium, this led to a considerable transfer of knowledge and skills among the four partners. Standards rose in all four institutions as competences and ideas were pooled on a regular basis.

- The absence of an overweening power center. The informality, mutual reliability, fairness, and the integrative, collaborative, and shared leadership led to a genuinely responsive attitude. The climate allowed local interests to flourish without compromising the interests of other partners. Given that the ownership of the system was vested in Alpha, and that the others were fee-paying participants, this was a potentially divisive situation which could have damaged the entire enterprise and produced undesirable side effects in all four libraries.

The downside of the experience was felt to be that it was utterly dependent on the personalities of those involved and that the system was unlikely to have lasted its natural span if any one of the library directors had left. This was never put to the test, so for those involved the experience remained a valid demonstration of the way the virtual environment could be used to produce mutually satisfactory results. These results were felt to have been achieved through a minimal reliance on structure and a considerable investment of time and thought in learning to make the best of electronic communication while overcoming the disadvantages.

Part 2

Managing People in
Contemporary Libraries

Chapter 4

Skills for Managing and Learning

It is a deceptively easy matter to specify the skills needed to make libraries work in the 21st century, and a number of writers have done this. Raitt (1997), with a list of about ten pages, is one example of many commentators who have assayed a prescriptive itemization.

It is also easy to assert that technology has led to significant changes in the skills mix, but the situation in practice is more complicated. A combination of a number of factors is effecting changes in the way we think about skills, and at the moment we live in a kind of half-light where there is some ambivalence about what skills are needed. This extends to the way in which priorities are established. Even comparatively recently, Harrison (2000) still felt able to define library skills in a traditional way, and from a practical point of view he may have been substantially right to do so at the time. Yet at about the same time, Wilder (2000) found it possible to identify a movement away from this traditional affirmation of the skills of acquisition, cataloging, organization, exploitation, and cooperation in the management of library materials. Cutting (2002) identified the obvious growth in demand for IT skills, with a commensurate decline in demand for the traditional skills of the library and information professional. Pugh (2004) also found that a significant proportion of library managers were still putting a premium on some of the traditional skills of leadership.

What is causing these changes is also a moot point. Skills requirements are changing for a number of likely reasons:

- They could be concomitant upon technological developments.
- The opening up of new markets for potential professional librarians is

contributing to a new emphasis.
- Changes in the approach to users, brought on by a better understanding of customer service concepts, could also be a factor.

Some writers see the present situation as an opportunity to develop additional skills and also note the increasing propensity of library managers to appoint staff without formal qualifications in information studies. This is in fact something that, in academic libraries at least, was almost the norm fifty years ago. It then became less common in the face of the widespread development and recognition of professional qualifications, before once again becoming a discernable and documented trend in the 1980s and early 1990s (Pugh, 1997). That this renaissance took place at the same time as the most rapid advance in the influence of technology in libraries may or may not be a coincidence, but the contribution of ICT (information and communications technology) experts from within universities and from the world of business is now established. Yet to say that technology offers an opportunity for the acquisition of new skills is only half the story.

The Influence of Technology

The impact of new technology on librarianship has been a strange mix of the trivial and the profound. Multicolored pyrotechnics have been followed by the dampest of squibs. Potentially the most powerful of liberating forces, the release of organizational energy that might be expected from technology has yet to be witnessed. This is largely because librarianship is still applying the lessons and learning of the past to a rapidly changing situation.

An impressive level of technological expertise means that in some ways everything is changing: everything, that is, except people's mind-sets. Sophisticated technology with the capacity to support a networked approach to organizational design exists alongside thinking that still leads to compartmentalization. Specialization still leads to the erection of barriers between parts of the organization that ought to be linked in a symbiotic relationship partly based on the unifying power of the technology. For skills development, the application of technology should help bring freedom. It can be a force for the physical reconfiguration of organizations. This should theoretically make it easier to move around an organization, to apply new skills where they are relevant, and to capitalize on multiskilling. It will involve attitude change, and will power a shift away from viewing professional development as the acquisition of a series of core competencies.

There is no argument about the enormous transformational power of technology in information services, or about the way in which it is raising the quality of many features of library services. One of the dangers in the present emphasis on the ICT aspects of librarianship is that, almost inadvertently, it tends to downplay the importance of the information carried inside people's heads. Tacit knowledge, in the form of the personal attitudes and feelings referred to by Allee (2002) and quoted later in this chapter, can only be passed on by human interaction. An overemphasis on the technological components of contemporary libraries could lead to this kind of knowledge being confined within the individuals that possess it.

Communication in organizations will continue to be a combination of technology and face-to-face interaction. This is going to lead to a strengthening of things like the informal networks referred to in chapter 3, and of structural features like teams (see chapters 8, and 9). These are features that need acquired skills if they are to be used to their best effect. Once again, the question of changes in attitude will also be relevant.

Some ideas expressed in this respect are old-fashioned and non-technological, and we can add to them. For example, the social component in communication will actually become more important in the technological organization than it was in the pretechnology days. A number of commentators have noted the need for people to talk about work. Others have raised issues about the problems of duplicating the human and personal aspects of communication when ICT provides the main channels. There is also evidence of the need for human interchanges on the part of students studying by distance learning methods, or following courses based on open learning techniques. All of these involve ancient skills that nevertheless do not come naturally and still have to be learned. If we start to write these out of our training programs, or subordinate them to learning about the bits and pieces of technology, we will devalue the most important resource in the library—the staff. In a different guise, this is the same argument as that advanced by metadata and Dublin Core enthusiasts who believe that traditional cataloging skills are no longer needed.

Deskilling

The introduction of technology in many areas is considered to be the precursor of a reduction in skills levels: As tasks become automated the input of human intelligence and discretion is reduced. In information services this effect has only been seen at the margins. Arguably, most of the impact of technology has been to further reduce, or even eliminate, the skills requirements in areas that were already felt to be routine, or perhaps should have been regarded as routine in some cases. Much of the management of journal collections, while practiced by professionals, may fall into this category. The further deskilling of routine tasks is demonstrated by the development of automated circulation systems, and by some other areas where clerical or paraprofessional staff work. These changes are opportunities for retraining and role change, but whether or not they actually lead to a redeployment of staff resources is a moot point. Given that organization development now depends on learning and on the nurturing of a multiskilled workforce, then making use of the leeway offered by what should be looked at as a freeing of capacity rather than a deskilling, ought to be a managerial priority.

At the same time, some of the traditional skills are undoubtedly being devalued. This is particularly true of our favorite example, that of cataloging. Lancaster (2003) makes a spirited defense of the role of cataloging and classification in the digital age and attests the relevance of both the traditional skills and the ability of the cataloger to develop and deploy new skills. Terris (2003), on the other hand, traces the decline of skills in this area with acuity. Expertise in cataloging also brings widespread benefits of a more general nature, such as attention to detail, clarity, and analysis. Nevertheless, it seems to be fairly clear that, in the face of technological advance, there will be a loss of skills and a loss of professionalism.

This may not be compensated for by the increase in technological expertise. Short of the complete rewriting of library school syllabi, allied to significant changes on the ground, this particular problem is intractable.

Specialization

Hand in hand with this development, there has been an obvious increase in specialization through the introduction of new technology. Nobody can sensibly deny the inevitability of this, but what can be called into question is the way that it should be handled inside information services. As the growth of the electronic library escalated, the professional literature was filled with ideas about multiskilling, about the ideal combinations of traditional and professional skills, and about what was needed to achieve the "seamless web of information." Collier (1995) talked of the attitude of mind necessary to make this possible, and there have been some impressive efforts to translate this into the kind of learning that would make this vision a practical reality. There are examples of librarians moving into specialist IT areas, and of erstwhile IT specialists and other professionals making a reasonable attempt at managing organizations that embrace traditional library services and IT-based information services. What is needed is a pattern of skills development, or the emergence of an organizational structure, that will make the application of multiple skills a reality for the user and the librarian who possesses the skills.

The previous chapter outlines the ways that structures are still used to create barriers to the application of skills, to reinforce differences, and to maintain a specialized, function-based approach to delivery. Lancaster (2003) is the latest of a number of illustrious commentators who have referred to the way that a new language has grown up to describe things that librarians have always done. This mystique building is but another way of underpinning the illusion of a form of technical specialization that sets its practitioners apart. In what was once a comparatively transparent operation, this helps to create another impenetrable layer of expertise.

Faceless Partners

Some of the dynamic developments in modern librarianship have come from collaboration between people who never, or rarely, actually meet each other face-to-face. Virtual teams organize collaborative projects, journals are run in this way, research projects are similarly managed, and professional education is delivered to distance learners. Achieving the full potential of these alliances calls for a new set of skills. Making the best of this situation also depends on an organizational architecture that is significantly different from the prevailing structures of most information services. By implication this also requires radically different skills to make it work. Cross (2003) describes the use of social network analysis to assess the effectiveness of the design of an organization. He emphasizes the fact that the physical location is the single most important factor in collaboration. The problem is that the knowledge, skills, expertise, and experience available in distributed locations will not become widely available without a conscious analysis of what makes distributed networks effective. This should be matched by the consequent development of appropriate skills. There is therefore a skills deficiency that does not augur well for a profession that is undoubtedly looking forward to more collaboration and more distributed working.

This comment is also applicable to the internal organization of libraries. Where IT services, library services, media services, and other academic support services are united only at an administrative level, and are allowed to operate within a bureaucratic structure that divides rather than integrates, then organizational creativity cannot flourish. The barriers between the vital face-to-face contact can be as strong in physically adjacent parts of an organization as they can in widely distributed organizations.

The problem is highlighted by the results of Cross's own research

(2003). This indicates key differences between organizations that achieve truly integrated networks and those that fail to utilize all the resources available within the system. There are differences in managerial behavior generally, and in human resource management. Significantly, virtual teamworking and integrated networks only become a reality as far as resource and information sharing is concerned when there is face-to-face contact in addition.

The general position is a little more complicated in the view of some writers. Marcum (2003) notes the problems of what he calls digital collaboration, and Zafeiriou (2003) makes some interesting points about text-based computer conferencing. While his research suggests that participants in computer conferencing appear to be more ready to disagree with each other than when taking part in face-to-face events, the incidence of major arguments appeared to diminish. He suggests that the reasons for the former lie in the absence of the social element in the exchanges and the lack of nonverbal cues to behavior and attitudes. Equally, the same elements create an air of detachment and a lack of awareness of the reality of the events. This means that full-scale confrontation becomes less likely. It may be, therefore, that electronic communication with distant partners would actually be good for collaboration. The impact of organizational diversity referred to in the earlier chapters could be enhanced because it occurs in a less threatening arena.

There are implications in these findings for managerial attitudes, and there are also echoes of the ideas explored in chapter 3, where Morgan's discussion of the organization as brain (1997) touched on the ideas of ambiguity and redundancy, and in particular the idea of sharing responsibility for specific projects. For Morgan this represented a significant advance in the application of skills. Cross came to the same conclusion when he compared a distributed organization that was deemed to be strong on cohesion with one that he assessed to be weak on cohesion. He found that the more cohesive organization recognized that

> although it might have been more efficient to assign one person to a project for six months rather than two persons for six months each, the latter approach produced a bigger long-term payoff . . . human resource practices were different across the two groups, despite a firmwide set of HR policies . . . . the cohesive e-group looked for evidence of collaborative behavior in job candidates, whereas the fragmented group was much more focused on past individual achievement . . . the more cohesive group took the peer feedback process seriously, which influenced advancement and compensation decisions . . . the more fragmented group focused on billable hours and

revenue generation . . . thereby sending a very clear signal as to what employees should be doing with their limited time.

(Cross, 2003)

The beneficial effects of assigning staff to projects on a shared basis tends to bear out Morgan's view (1997) that organizational redundancy is good for creativity. Moreover, it has to be repeated that the same strictures can be applied to working across internal organizational boundaries. There are implications here for both managers and managed, in terms of attitude change, cultural change, organizational learning, and skills development. It can be inferred that organizational structures not only influence the way that skills are applied but also to some extent the sort of skills recruiters look for in the first instance. Cohesive teams take a different view of skills and aptitudes from those that lack such cohesion, and this is probably true also at organizational level.

Collaborating with the Enemy

In spite of an honorable history of interlibrary collaboration with the aim of improving services for users, it has been argued elsewhere in this text that, inside libraries and their parent organizations, competition has long been a key characteristic that is a potential threat to organizational health. Electronic libraries and digitization make this worse. Chapter 1 identified competition as a primary characteristic of the bureaucratic organizational form, where generalized battles for resources, influence, and power are mirrored by competition at an individual level. At the level of the organization, the library is a competing element alongside other services, and is pitted against academic departments in universities and colleges.

We are learning to respond to the increasingly powerful impetus and to collaborate with commercial information providers, for example. The emphasis on access and resource sharing will grow and continue to feed more and more cooperative efforts. Both of these wholly positive trends depend on something more than the kind of collaboration that allowed management boards representing all the partners to oversee the work of staff who belonged exclusively to the project. Collaboration needs to work where it is hardest to achieve it, at lower levels in the organization. The case study in the previous chapter is a small-scale example of how to secure serious collaboration between staff who are not under unified command.

Developing virtual libraries will lead to similar situations, whether they are within orthodox libraries or distributed. In both cases they will be part of networks that share resources, skills, and costs, and will eventually become virtual organizations. These integrated networks, described in chapter 2 and chapter 8, will not only encounter the communication problem referred to above. Their success will also depend on solving the problems of creating a genuine team ethos, making the virtual team work, and creating common cause. At the same time they will have to maintain a healthy sense of difference between the constituent parts.

This will not be a mere matter of reinforcing and developing the skills of negotiation and collaboration, and bringing out an understanding of team dynamics, team learning, and self-management. It involves major behavioral and attitude change, and the latter is the most difficult change to achieve. Translate this into internal organizational needs and consider the desirability of replacing all the obvious forms of individual competition with a more sharing, less aggressive attitude, one which is less fixated on ownership, and the magnitude of the task becomes clearer.

The skills required will center on attitude change. They will include the willingness to work with ideas that might theoretically "belong" to other people, and not just to work with other people's collections of resources. Marquandt and Kearsley (1999) emphasize the ability to nourish a culture that sees development as something involving everybody—erstwhile competitors, commercial suppliers, and users. This will only happen in an organizational environment where relationships, in a team culture with a multidisciplinary emphasis, are more equal. There will be less evidence of the conventional difference between managers and managed, and eventually internal boundaries will come down. This will lead to the sort of fuzzy definition of responsibilities pinpointed by Morgan (1997) and advocated in chapter 3.

Managerial Changes

Managers today are probably in a far stronger position to manage creatively and imaginatively than ever before. The liberating power of technology has been referred to earlier in this chapter. Flexibility comes because IT enables less obvious—yet still effective—control of organizations. Management information systems are now extremely flexible and are comprehensive in their coverage. They possess a far greater degree of sophistication, making it easier for managers to see more clearly what is happening inside the organization and to monitor changes in the external environment. Information is more easily shared, and the information system permits the development of devolved or "local" management. By this is meant the exercise of power and the acceptance of responsibility at the lowest possible point. This is usually the point where there is the greatest impact on customer service.

The biggest shift of all will be seen in managerial attitudes. Ghoshal and Bartlett (1998) record changes in managerial practices and beliefs starting with the growth of the "professional manager" in the multidivisional corporations set up in the early 20th century. They chart progress from an emphasis on the skills of planning and managing resources, of which personnel were seen as just another type of accountable item, to the supremacy of the "organizational man." This manager relied on centralized policies, procedures, and control systems. These regulated operations that were based on employees acting as "replaceable parts in an efficient production process." To managers, people became as "predictable and controllable as the capital resources they must manage"—echoes of Weber's cogs in a machine. This meant that the premium managerial skills were technical ones. The argument is that this approach is no longer possible nor desirable. Neither will the exercise of centralized power working within well-defined areas of responsibility continue to be a natural and preordained way to manage. Managers now have to learn not only to live with ambiguity, but to embrace it as a creative force.

It is well established that staff working with technology show a preference for consultative management, greater involvement in decision making, and a greater measure of devolved power. The increasing tendency of libraries to appoint well-qualified professionals to clerical and paraprofessional posts, and developments in the professional education of librarians, will reinforce this as the standards of education rise. More and more staff at ostensibly lower levels of the organization will want to exercise their imaginations and apply their talents more widely, and the organization itself will need this wider input. Managers will have to learn to share responsibility with a diverse, increasingly well-qualified, and competent workforce. The inculcation of the habits of innovative thinking will be important and will only come from sharing responsibility and encouraging adaptability.

The definition of management as "the art of getting things done through people," although coined almost 100 years ago (Follett, 1918), is still germane to the issue of managerial skills. Living up to this definition depends on creating the conditions under which people can perform to their maximum capabilities across a very wide range of roles. However, fashioning the circumstances that enable a manager to get things done through people is a different matter in the hybrid environment. It depends first on designing a radically different organization that will provide a supportive structure for a wide range of roles, skills, and processes. It will also have to accommodate differences, and contemporary organizations are not yet geared up to do this. There are a number of development issues to be considered in relation to skills needs.

Creating the optimum organization for information services involves a combination of skills. Some of these skills will be exercised in ways that break with the past. The basic organization of a library still depends on the grouping together of similar skills and on differentiating between skills: technical or operational skills that predominate at the bottom of the organization, reporting skills that are considered to be crucial for middle managers, strategic and policy-making skills, still largely confined to the top of the organization. The communication processes will inevitably continue to mimic this hierarchical structure.

The application of technology to libraries is unfortunate in its execution, in the sense that it has often led to an increase in the number of managers. This strengthening of the internal barriers has been compounded by a stiffening of the vertical fissures as library organizations accommodate the new divisions of electronic information. It is now beneficial and necessary, in the interests of organizational creativity, to shatter this carefully constructed specialization based on keeping like with like. Instead it would be beneficial to bring together opposites, discordant traditions, varying viewpoints, complementary skills, and contrasting education and training backgrounds. This underlines the need for huge shifts in attitude and behavior.

Knowledge Architecture

This is interpreted as a conceptual framework that guides the development of the learning process. This conceptual framework has a number of components that have to be present if the approach is to work.

- Commitment to the individual: In learning terms, this establishes individual development as a priority and dictates some of the tactical or operational moves in bolstering learning. It emphasizes coaching and mentoring as means of developing individual talent and the knowledge base. These depend on enabling structures, empowerment, and devolved management.
- Unity of strategy, policy, and operation: Effective libraries rely on creating and sustaining the ability and knowledge to deliver the service. Planning may include strategy, objective setting, and policy, but implementation depends on skills, aptitudes, and prowess. Knowledge architecture holds out the promise of developing a strong link between strategy and implementation.
- Responsibility taken by the individual: The organization can provide

support, but individuals have to share responsibility for what and how they learn.

- Team responsibility for development: This can be understood as learning from peers, supervisors, and group learning processes. It will again have resource implications, and implications for the way learning is managed.

- A focus on learning from work: Tying in with the observations about enabling structures, empowerment, and management styles, a commitment to learning from work can reflect the organizational commitment to the individual.

- A facilitation process: Learning opportunities for individuals and groups must be provided, and staff must learn how to identify these opportunities for themselves as they control their own learning. The technique of handling the opportunities must be absorbed and a learning cycle established (see chapters 5 and 6).

- Managed learning: Both organizational and individual needs must be established. Individual and group learning must be supported by the formal development program and based on matching the needs of the individual and the organization. The function of formal learning and the formal controls used by managers will not diminish, but will change. Although the argument of this book is that most of the learning in libraries takes place in an informal way and is not immediately visible to management, there has to be a symmetry between the formal and informal learning systems. This will depend on
  - The development of the learning subsystem
  - The information system or technical infrastructure
  - Changes in management styles (see chapters 7 and 8)

- Ensuring the fit (Gouillart and Kelly, 1995): There must be a permanent process of assessment. This will ensure that new skills and expertise will be developed and applied where they are of most value to individuals and to the library service. In team organizations, it may mean revising views on career progression. Job enrichment, job enlargement, and empowerment might mean that conventional ideas about a steady and planned climb up the bureaucratic ladder will no longer be relevant. There might be a need to accept that, instead of this, development could be seen as moving across an organization. Equally, salary improvements could be tied to specific learning outcomes. The idea of responsibility will be looked at in a different way. Personnel procedures in team-based organizations will reflect these ideas through techniques such as generic job descriptions and the formal measurement of team effect.

Changing the organizational structure in the ways outlined above, and examined in more detail in chapter 3, has to include a new way of looking at systems, and in particular the organizational learning system. Information is still being organized by people and being turned into knowledge by people. Even without the need to deal with conventional information and the inconvenient persistence of users of all types who consistently prefer to handle printed material as a matter of choice, there will be a need for conventional human resource management. It may also be true that even when we reach a full state of technological grace, people skills will still be needed, and human intelligence will be called upon to deal with complex issues.

One of the great strengths of the network is that it makes it easier for more staff to be involved in decisions and processes that were once controlled by a few. The corollary is that managers must learn the skills of managing the virtual and the actual team or group, particularly when this is growing in the context of a learning organization. In particular, managers will become managers of staff learning—and coaches and learners themselves.

The key skills involved in these roles are as much a part of organizational knowledge sharing as the networks that now support knowledge management, but 21st century libraries will be fast-moving, their shapes will eventually become flatter, more information will become available, and learning needs will increase. This will accentuate the changes in managerial roles and the skills shift.

Creativity

One of the key concepts in the design of hybrid organizations is that of creativity (see chapter 2). It is also one of the key concepts underpinning learning in contemporary organizations. The term can be taken to mean the generation of novel solutions to problems and the encouragement and application of original thinking. We can expect change at an increasing pace, and libraries will face what are for them unique challenges. We can also expect to continue to work in an unpredictable environment where existing tenets of management may not be applicable and where different perspectives and a multifaceted approach to organizational development will be necessary. The 21st century library could be a fecund seedbed for creativity because of its potential for bringing together different approaches to information provision, different professions, different traditions, and different ways of working. Even assuming the achievement of the degree of organizational development required to create this cross-fertilization, the task of managing creativity is extraordinarily difficult, and it is one that has not been high on the agenda of most managers. Nevertheless, the speed of change will demand new and quick responses to challenges. Organizational problem solving and organizational learning will be important. Gryskiewicz and Taylor (2003) comment on the need for managers to find "original and helpful solutions," and deal with the difficult task of managing creativity and generating creative solutions. The implementation of structural change is an essential part of developing a framework for creativity, and it forms an important component in organizational development. These authors still argue that creativity needs positive management if it is to become a relevant part of organizational development, claiming the need to learn how to

- Restate the problem in a way that opens up the possibility of generating many answers.
- Deliberately guide the process and deploy a balanced strategy, with a choice between an incremental approach to secure improvements without fundamentally altering the approach and a "breakaway" approach that encourages unorthodoxy.
- Allow staff to develop their own strategies and techniques for creativity.
- Contribute insights and information from their standpoint as senior managers working with the political and financial realities of the organization.
- Put in place a series of practical steps for generating ideas.
- Include creativity as part of the organizational learning system.
- Inculcate the habit of evaluating the range of creative ideas emerging in the organization.
- Establish working guidelines.
- Make creativity a part of organizational processes.
- Put the results into practice.

In essence, the managerial skills for fostering creativity will be founded on building an organization that links people together rather than separates them with increasingly unjustifiable, ineffective, and inefficient internal barriers. The results will be seen in the freedom and the ability to analyze what is being done in the working situation and to interpret and apply the results of this thinking. Managerial skills needed to refocus the organization and the staff emphasize learning, the encouragement of alternative thinking, and innovation. There will also be a call for coaches, mentors, and managers who empower others.

Reinvigorating Old Skills

Similar observations can be made with respect to the traditional management skills in general. If it is correct to predict that organizations will be fluid, with an all-pervading flow of information, there will be implications for planning skills, including strategy, policy, and budgeting. It is possible, for example, to anticipate and hope for a more streamlined approach with increasingly shorter planning cycles because of faster updating of information and the absorption of new information into the system.

Broadening the Use of Managerial Skills

Working in a situation where information flows freely through an organization and where decentralized management contributes to role enhancement, some skills seen as mainly relevant to managers will be more widely subscribed to. Decision-making skills will be used at all levels of the organization, but this will be only one feature of a new emphasis in staff development.

Partly because involvement and collaboration extend the timescale, it is also possible to foresee a wider input into planning processes. With structural change, stark separations between strategic, tactical, and operational planning will become meaningless. The need for fundamental changes in managerial attitude will extend to the acceptance of new ideas about ownership of key functions. It will no longer be possible to exist comfortably within a conventional construction of managerial responsibilities. Instead, these will be have to be shared. In turn, there are again massive implications for organizational learning.

The devolution of control that will be essential in the technologically dependent, rapidly changing organizations of the future will also need skills of a different character. It can be expected that facilitating, mentoring, and guiding will assume a much greater importance because of the nature of the environment. Training and learning will also be delivered in part by technology, which will increase the need for basic IT skills.

A New Approach to Learning

Organizational learning in stable organizations is based on learning from experience. Lessons are absorbed from what has happened in the recent past and from older experiences that are lodged in the organizational memory bank and have become part of the organizational culture. They are experiences that color the approach to contemporary problems. This kind of adaptive learning—changing through experience—will obviously continue to be important, but it will have an additional dimension.

When the organizational environment is changing quickly, this mindset has to be supplemented by a more flexible, forward-looking attitude. The kind of learning skills that will be at a premium are those to do with looking into the future. They will include scenario building, reflection, and analysis, as well as creativity. The ability to learn, and crucially the mastery of the skills of self-learning, will be cardinal skills in organizations that will be characterized by rapid change.

Communication Skills for Managers

The communication skills of the manager will also require a radical overhaul. Much has already been written about the shortcomings of e-mail and the perils of this type of communication, but the problem goes much further than that. Managerial communication in organizations that will be networked internally and externally will be as much influenced by technology as any other aspect of organizational life. Notwithstanding the comments made earlier about the increased efficiency of virtual teams if an element of face-to-face communication is maintained, virtual meetings and virtual committees will become well-established features of operations. Brewerton (2002) identifies procedures and skills for virtual meetings that are naturally markedly different from the standard skills of face-to-face communication. It might well be impossible to make up for the disadvantage of losing the information gained from body language and the loss of the personal contact element in building rapport and teamwork (Cross 2003), but some procedural and organizational skills, not always expertly deployed in conventional situations, become even more important when the exchanges are between remote parties:

- Concise expression.
- The ability to précis and produce timely summaries in order to build up the context of a meeting and help participants remain focused.
- Procedural systems for maintaining the impetus of a meeting or cyber conference, maintaining order, and keeping an accurate record.
- The development of considered and temperate habits of electronic communication, and the avoidance of what is apparently called flaming.
- Interacting in cyberspace calls for a conscious and mature approach to communication in order to keep track of issues and questions raised, and to respond logically and in a considered fashion. The various kinds of groupware relevant to this problem will be of use.

- Avoiding the superficial. In the absence of personal contact, it is difficult to develop a deeper engagement with individuals rather than issues.

One unresolved difficulty to do with communication skills in the virtual organization will be that of exploiting the personal knowledge locked up
inside individuals. Allee (2003) remarks on the assumption that "tacit
knowledge" refers to what is locked up in people's heads, but points out
that it is much more significant because it is

> innate intelligence, perception, and capacities for reasoning—rather than a
> type of memory or knowledge store . . . [it] could never be made explicit,
> nor does it need to be . . . tacit knowledge sharing underlies *any* act of com-
> munication, in the form of unspoken commonalities around very basic per-
> ceptions and human interaction.
>
> (Allee, 2003)

For this kind of communication, there will be no substitute for the skills
of face-to-face communication, and here there is another problem. The
analysis of communication in organizations tends to emphasize the technical aspects of creating, transmitting, and receiving a message. The process
also has a vital human dimension and starts long before this with the building of relationships that help develop understanding and mutual empathy.
These are the features that lubricate the cogs of the process, and they depend
on more general relationships between individuals. In the hybrid environment, where business activities might be distributed and many things may
be electronically based, this is even more difficult to achieve. The point
underlines the absolute necessity, in the digital environment, of actively
maintaining personal relationships. This is particularly applicable to cross-
boundary relationships and relationships between members of different
professional groups.

Middle Management

Middle management will be transformed and become unrecognizable,
if not indiscernible, from other roles. Existing functions will be lodged
lower down the organization, and those who survive will take a broader and
more creative view of their roles.

The repercussions of this reduction in middle management will be seen
at lower levels. A desirable attitude change here will involve a willingness
to dump the comfortable reliance on the bureaucracy and accept empowerment and the responsibility that goes with this. Some skills once seen as the

province of senior management will be dispersed throughout the organiza-tion. The skills of leadership, and the learning functions of all staff, will again be emphasized, amounting to further evidence of the need to learn new ways of working and to seek attitude change. Teamwork skills will be at a premium, as will the talents needed for networking. It is to middle man-agers that organizations will look in the first instance for the development of the leadership role and the use of appropriate leadership skills, although these will be exercised in a multiple leader situation where once again new skills will be required to deal with the electronic environment.

At the Center of the Action: Professional Skills

The potential for changing the roles of staff at lower levels in the organ-ization will be underlined as access to more and more information about what the organization is doing becomes possible at the base of the pyramid. While this will depend on the ability of management to recognize not only the possibility of more openness but also its vital significance in rapidly changing organizations, it still opens up a vista of more effective management through the contribution of informed inputs from staff with different but relevant perspectives. The new skills to be learned here will be about

- Contributing to strategy and policy
- Using budgetary information
- Generally accepting the disciplined application of self-management and empowerment

In the Wider World: Staff and Users

The portfolio man is already upon us and has been for many years. This book is being written by one. There is a small but growing community of contract, part-time, or casual workers contributing their expertise to library services from locations sometimes far removed from the physical location of the library. There appears to be no reason to think that Handy (1995) was wrong when he identified the locating of more and more work outside the organization, yet within the profession we show little urgency in recogniz-ing the implications, and golden opportunities, of this development.

While we are technically capable of dealing with the phenomenon of the outworkers, we pay scant attention to the need to give them the skills required to develop a structured and productive approach to self management outside the workplace. Individuals are left to acquire the new skills of self-organization in this context. Remote users are also becoming an issue where there is a need to develop new skills.

The Implications of Different User Demands

The user of the hybrid library is going to differ significantly from the conventional library user. Computer-literate users could conceivably develop a more muscular approach to the provision of their information needs. It will not be necessary to wait too long before the arrival of the user who is competent enough, and sufficiently assured, to bypass the librarian completely. The ability to become involved in the creation of personalized information packages and virtual personal libraries is already there. Under these circumstances, the dialog between user and librarian is even more crucial. The skills involved here are not systematically developed in conventional librarianship, so they are worth underlining.

Dialog

Senge (1993) still exerts a primary influence on this issue. Dialog is a nonconfrontational process of exploring ideas in a systematic attempt to understand what the other person means and what he or she needs. Janes (2003) makes much the same point in his examination of the nature of reference work in the digital age. Seeing skills requirements as a combination of old and new ideas, he offers the solution in a graphic manner:

> Figure out what we can do that Google can't or won't, do that as well as it can be done, publicize the bejesus out of it, and reinvigorate the professional role of reference librarians in the popular mind and our own self-image.

This is more than an appropriate and pithy piece of advice to reference librarians—as Janes (2003) says elsewhere in his book, it is a clarion call to all librarians, and he goes on to outline the new skills we need in the same pungent style. The same author also pinpoints the necessary attitude change, comparing the circumstances in which skills were adapted to meet a previous technological development:

> We did adopt the telephone as a means of answering questions, but it was discussed in the professional literature on and off for over two decades. Is the ground more fertile now for technological innovation? Why?
>
> (Janes, 2003)

Equality of Treatment

One of the problems raised in relation to the skills issue in the hybrid library is that of equal treatment of all users. Resources are now permanently accessible to remote users, provided there is an opac, and as long as they do not need the out-of-hours support of a librarian in the flesh. One of the biggest challenges to do with skills is not so much how to acquire the skills to organize and bring together digital and paper resources, but how to ensure that users relying on unmediated electronic access receive equal treatment. The question is what skills and procedures can be developed to compensate for the absence of the face-to-face element and for the user who needs the intuitive intervention of a librarian? And what about the user who would not only benefit from being directed to appropriate resources but would profit from engaging in a small-scale learning process revolving around some of the finer points of literature searching, Web searching, or some qualitative judgment on the sources being handled?

Technology obviously provides part of the answer in the use of chat rooms, instant messaging, call center systems, or videoconferencing (Janes, 2003). There are protocols to be learned for all of these. Although none of them will totally reproduce the conditions of face-to-face exchanges between users and librarians, they will go some way toward overcoming the most acute disadvantages of losing face-to-face communication.

The correct use of e-mail is also a compensatory factor. Asynchronous communication, as the literature would have us say, but in other words via e-mail, gets a bad press in some quarters. Has nobody ever written a letter to a library and received a full answer to a complex query by post and without meeting a librarian? If so, what is the real difference between this and an e-mail or Web query? Given the fact that at least some of the skills of the face-to-face interview, dialog, and questioning will actually transfer reasonably well to this arena, it seems a profitable avenue to investigate. Experience in supporting distance learners and open learners via e-mail indicates that it is in fact a feasible medium for exploring and satisfying information needs. Most chat rooms, if they do nothing else, will demonstrate a dialog, even if it is with the devil.

What is more, if a Web form is properly constructed, it can duplicate the structured questioning approach adopted by most librarians working inside the library. Other organizations, particularly in customer-facing commercial services, are leading the field in becoming increasingly competent in the design of Web forms that actually provide reliable and useful information. Some libraries are doing the same.

In a more general sense, it has been argued by several contributors that there will be a shift in the emphasis placed on various techniques as far as reference work is concerned. In the digital world, or the half-digital version we will live in, the thrust is going to be even more directed at actually helping users understand the true nature of their information need. This is described as problem solving by some authorities. One of the things it means is putting the needs of the distance user on the same footing as everyone else.

To end this section with a more general point, user expectations have changed considerably. In common with other areas of society, information service customers have become more aware of their rights and more conscious of their power. Whether they are right or wrong, as Pantry and Griffiths (2003) point out, they believe the Web offers them a valid alternative to libraries. Eventually, they might prove to be correct in this. This not only opens up the issue of new skills, but it underlines the need for better performance of the old skills and for the continual refinement of ability in negotiation, collaboration, and communicating with other people.

The skills question cannot be handled in isolation: it is obviously connected to organizational learning, which in turn is predicated on structural change. This leads inevitably to the considerations of chapters 5 and 6, where the implications of new forms of leadership and management roles are discussed and bring their own new skills requirements.

The Misnomer of Change Management

It is understandable that lists of the skills needed by the manager of the 21st century library include a mandatory reference to change management. The pace of technological change is increasing, and some aspects of digitization and electronic information services would have been almost beyond the conception of practicing managers at the time of the earlier high water marks of change management in information services.

We are moving into a situation where at least half of an operational library may have no physical characteristics. In some cases, an increasing percentage of the resources could exist only as digital artifacts and might be owned by someone elsewhere. Some of the workers, and a large number of the users, might never be seen within 100 miles of the library building, so Charles Handy's shamrock organization (1995) and Clutterbuck and Kernaghan's chemical soup (1994) seem increasingly appropriate organizational models.

This chapter has already touched on the difficulty of dealing with queries posed by users who cannot be seen. The difficulties of dealing with staff who may be constantly changing, who might be portfolio people with more than one job, more than one set of loyalties, more than one set of deadlines, and the usual mix of motivation and degrees of commitment, can compound the managerial problem. Add to the mix Drucker's statement (2002) that there are "no cure-alls, the ostensibly 'infallible' tools and techniques," and there is a substantial case for saying that we need to move away from the idea that there is a set of techniques that will equip a manager to "manage" change. This is almost akin to the classical theorists' search for the "one best way" to manage.

The point that there is no empirical evidence to support the view that any one approach to management is more effective than any other was made earlier. This does not mean that there are not better or worse ways of dealing with specific situations, but simply that it is impossible to test the effectiveness of any management theory against any other in a controlled working situation where like can be measured against like in identical circumstances and conditions.

It has often been said that change requires the learning of new skills throughout the organization (for example Katzenbach, 1996). In the virtual environment, or the mixed economy of the virtual/traditional information service, one of the essential skills of all staff is not in learning to manage change. This writer is now inclined to argue that this is impossible and misleading to suggest that change can be managed. What is more important, and different, is learning to live in the state of constant flux that all change, and digital innovation in particular, produces.

The skills of change management have become, at least in theory, part of a conventional approach to management. So much has been said about them that, at the very least, lip service is paid to most of the ideas by most library managers. They could be set out as

- Leadership
- Teamwork
- Organizational learning
- Decentralization
- Devolved management styles
- Flexible structures

The difficulty is that in the electronic environment all of the skills involved in the list above assume different forms, and they are made different by the inescapable facts of the virtual environment in which they are deployed. The next chapter looks at leadership in this virtual environment.

We are left with one further issue. The skills problem is related to other developments. The approach to managing hybrid libraries is based on restructuring, teamwork, empowerment, communication, utilizing technology, and learning. What this does in the long term is turn more and more librarians into managers. It is inadequate to encourage people to learn new skills, or to give them the space to organize their own work, without providing them with the essential managerial skills. It would be logical then to include management skills in a broad package of necessary skills at all levels of the organization. Even if the skills are infrequently used, their possession will create a greater understanding of the management perspectives that inform decision making and color the general life of the organization. The idea of management as a broad-based function is considered in chapter 6, on the player manager.

Chapter 5

Leadership

Leadership can be simply described as the skill of influencing people in order to achieve objectives. To go a little further, leadership is to do with attempts to exert influence over a group of people in the workplace in order to achieve organizational objectives. To put it more bluntly still, it has been defined as possessing the ability to ensure that people do things they might not necessarily want to. This leaves considerable room for maneuver where styles and methods are concerned.

Attempts to explain what leadership is, or what leaders do, usually rely on one of three basic theories. This book is not really about the theory of leadership as such, but it is necessary to understand the theoretical background in order to mount a reasoned critique of its relevance to modern organizations.

The Trait Approach

This is one of the earliest approaches to leadership, and emphasizes the characteristics that make leaders stand out and that distinguish them from others. While it has proved enticing to many, it has been attacked by a number of writers. For example, Stogdill (1974) and Bass (1981) in a later revision of his research, although broadly advancing the argument that traits were important, contended that leadership was considerably more than the exhibiting of certain characteristics. It involved other factors such as the working situation and relationships. Bennis (1984) also identified traits in leaders. A summary of the position indicates that some key leaders' traits are shared by most leaders. It would be possible to generalize and say that the will to achieve, ambition, vitality, persistence, motivation, an urge for power, thinking and analytical skills, confidence, and integrity are shared. On the other hand, this will be modified by the circumstances in which leaders operate and the people they lead. Therefore a contingency view of leadership skills can also be taken.

The Behaviorist Approach

The obvious impracticality of accepting trait theory as a complete explanation of the leadership issue led partly to the emergence of the behaviorist school. Exemplified by the Ohio State University Leadership Studies program, this widely analyzed approach argued that there are two key behaviors in the exercise of leadership:

- Consideration, described as being concerned with effective communication and stressing the importance of supporting subordinates
- Initiating Structure, as a means of controlling the work of the group

The behaviorist approach also acknowledged the possibility that the actual situation in which leadership is practiced could have a bearing, so once again there was a degree of flexibility and subtlety in the position adopted.

The Contingency or Situational Approach

It is possible to take Consideration and Structure as two poles in behavior. This is a handy way of introducing the idea that leadership behavior might vary between those poles and that a number of factors could influence these variations. Characteristics such as

- The work situation—the particular task to be done, the general nature of the job, the circumstances under which it is carried out, and organizational characteristics
- The characteristics or the personality of the leader
- The characteristics of the subordinates, or those that are led

might well influence the way a leader operates.

To some extent, these factors combine the contingency theory of leadership and the behaviorist theory. Even taken together, they are not enough to explain the nature of leadership in modern organizations. The situational approach was developed by Hersey, Blanchard, and Natemayer (1979), to take in ideas about organizational power. It is now accepted that management in times of change calls for leadership that considers the situation, the characteristics of the leader, and the characteristics of the followers.

Leadership and Power

Two of the crucial things essential to any understanding of leadership in organizations are the way that power is exercised and consequently the way that decisions are taken. Together with the leader's personality, these elements are the most obvious indicators of leadership styles and behavior.

Power can be exercised in organizations in several ways, and the leader's use of power can be flexible, sometimes arbitrary, careless, and even whimsical. Even so, the wielding of power is still the most reliable guide to what a leader really thinks about leadership and about those who are led. It also sheds light on the view leaders take of their own position.

Expert Power

On the face of it, power based on expertise is likely to offer a reasonable means of exercising leadership in modern information services. We have never before seen such a concentration and variety of expertise in libraries, and this approach is particularly attractive to mature organizations. In a time of great change and flux, it may seem to be an inexactitude to call contemporary library services "mature." In this context, a mature organization is one that is characterized by the willingness of individuals to take responsibility for their own work, to accept responsibility for decision making, and to be accountable. Chapter 2 discusses the emergence, sometimes associated with technology, of groups of staff who are prepared to manage themselves. It also talks of a general improvement in organizational learning and training that better equips people for managing their own working situations. These are exactly the characteristics that are favorable to the use of expert power by leaders, so this could be seen as an opportune leadership style to adopt. It is also a potentially dangerous one.

Legitimate Power

The exercise of legitimate, legal, or coercive power is what we have long been used to in the kind of formal bureaucracies that libraries have been throughout most of their history. That is from the time they became big enough to shed the characteristics Mintzberg used to identify primitive organizations (1979). No doubt coercive power was used in some libraries long before that. It is a power that can be based on tradition, in the shape of an acceptance that the exercise of power is something that is the right of certain individuals. It can also stem from organizational position or the possession of office. Legitimate power can be described as the use of authority in ways that demand or assume specific responses from followers. Yet it is the kind of power that organizations might be expected to move away from as they develop the sort of flexibility that is necessary for effective library services in the 21st century.

Legitimate power is a combination of what Weber (1947) described as rational and traditional authority. It is rational because it calls for acceptance of the framework of rules and regulations devised to ensure that organizations run effectively. It is traditional because it is based on conventions and procedures that can be traced back to many managerial situations described throughout recorded history (see pages 23 and 143) . For most of the history of libraries it was just about the only kind of power known.

It is also irrational in that it now fails to take account of changing organizational environments, both internal and external. What we should be looking for is the kind of power that is based on influence.

Influential Power

Influential power is characterized by strong all-round motivational skills and the ability to develop and express a vision that others can share. It depends—perhaps dangerously so—on the possession of charisma. This is harnessed to the ability to persuade and to use participative and consultative procedures. It is a personal issue. The major descriptors of influential power include the following:

- It is based on individual characteristics, skills, and knowledge that others think are attractive and desirable.
- It depends on visionary skills—the ability to paint a picture of where the organization ought to go, how it should get there, what it should do and how it should change along the way.
- It is based on communication—in selling the vision, in motivating, in explaining the route the organization will take, in securing cooperation, in seeking and developing partnerships.
- It is a very visible form of leadership.
- It is a two way process—depending on leaders who can maintain connections with the rest of organization, do not fall prey to remoteness, and do not lose sight of the realities of life lower down the organization, where the vision has to be made real (Peters and Waterman, 1982).

- It involves charisma, a component of most leadership styles.
- It is more than the ability of a leader to persuade others to believe in what they are doing. It also embraces the often ignored necessity to persuade others to believe in themselves, and through that inspire them to achieve.

There is a clear argument that as organizations develop, they should move away from the use of legitimate or coercive power and move towards the exercise of power based on influence. One way of describing this is to view it as forces acting on a see-saw (fig. 5.1). As the power of change forces bear down on one end, the dead weight of coercive leadership is lifted and replaced by influential leadership at the other.

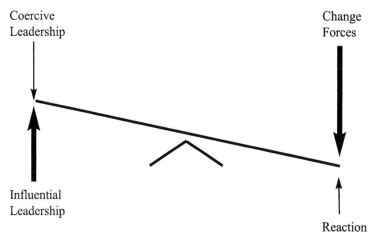

Coercive
Leadership

Change
Forces

Influential
Leadership

Reaction

Fig. 5.1 The Development of Influential Leadership

There is an implication that the growth of influential leadership would lead to greater job satisfaction and so more productivity. Hersey and Stinson (1980) expanded these ideas, and used a standard breakdown of leader personalities. They compared leaders who were task based, with an emphasis on control and achieving objectives, and those who were relationship based, with a predilection for motivation, influence, and individual responsibility. They also acknowledged the need to make strategies fit the circumstances.

There is also an argument that this behavior itself should actually vary. It should be dependent on perceptions of skills, abilities, and personal characteristics such as trust and reliability. Each relationship between a leader and a subordinate therefore becomes unique. By implication, this also means that the contributions made to the relationship by the subordinates will also vary—high quality relationships are mutual undertakings, and the higher the quality, the more responsibility subordinates are likely to accept and discharge (Liden and Graen, 1980).

In sum, perhaps the best way of looking at the development of influential leadership is to remember the see-saw and regard it as one of two broad forces acting on organizations. As organizations change in response to the range of influences acting upon them, and described in the early chapters of this book, so the force driving influential leadership as opposed to the reactionary idea of coercive leadership will increase.

Path Goal Theory

Path Goal Theory adds some more detail and finesse. Rooted in expectancy theory, it supposes that the effectiveness of leaders depends on motivational skills, in helping subordinates to identify and achieve personal and organizational goals, and in ensuring the satisfaction of various needs. It can be read as contingency theory, but with a greater emphasis on staff and worker satisfaction. Leadership behavior is

- Supportive, particularly where tasks are carried in stressful conditions
- Achievement orientated
- Concerned with performance
- Participative, with jointly set aims and objectives
- Often involving a significant degree of subordinate control over work

Leadership and Decision Making

A number of researchers have attempted to correlate leadership styles with decision-making processes. This aspect is obviously related to the exercise of power and the use of coercion.

Wiberg (1988) identified four distinct patterns of decision making, which can be summarized as follows.

Imaginative-Analytical

This is an approach in which leaders identify key issues and use conceptual processes and cognitive skills to arrive at a decision. It reflects a leadership style that relies on principles and theories and an underlying strategy that is appropriate for dealing with logical issues. Perhaps it is not so good when dealing with issues of personnel, or when operating in complex situations where there are major uncertainties.

Structured

This is practical, factually based, and bureaucratic. It places a premium on efficiency, but reflects a negative view of ambiguity and a low tolerance of uncertainty—not the kind of decision making appropriate for the organizations described in this book, it might be thought.

Traditional

Precedents dominate the decision-making process of traditionalists. Leaders inclining to this approach can act on the basis of strong personal convictions, take a generally positive view of individuals, and rely on a team approach.

Impulsive

Impulsive decision making is inspirational and unconventional. Personal and instinctive, it might be viewed as a natural form of leadership and decision making. It is leading by example, affirming the ability of followers, and investing in the ability of staff to become high achievers through effort.

As ever, there is an argument for a combination of styles in all leaders, and in practice Wiberg was one of a number of writers who identified this requirement. He saw the relevance of combinations of styles.

An amalgam of the Imaginative-Analytical with the Structured produced a decision-making style that was analytical and logical and was appropriate for working in a lean and austere organization.

Combining the Structural and the Traditional offered a practical and realistic style, while the Traditional allied to the Impulsive produced an aggressive, high-achieving style.

Working between the two poles of the Impulsive and the Imaginative-Analytical was considered to be good in situations where there was a demand for anticipation and some predictive skills as far as the future was concerned.

A balanced style calls for all-round strengths that encompass strategy, tactics, development, and entrepreneurial vision.

Choosing a particular style for a situation is but the first step. Its success then depends on the level of the skills of the followers, and their psychological readiness to accept a particular approach. This in its turn can be influenced by the charismatic quality of the leader, his or her ability to motivate, and the support and opportunity the organization can offer to the psychological growth of the people that work in it.

Apparently reactionary leadership styles are sometimes a response to a particular stage in the development of an individual or a group, and not necessarily an expression of a leader's preferred way of operating. There are, for example, times during the management of complex change processes where leaders will modify their styles to deal with particularly difficult situations. The same can be true of leaders attempting to handle serious situations involving personnel.

None of this detracts from the relevance of the situational or contingency approach to leadership in modern libraries. Nor does it undermine the general proposal that some form of participative leadership style allied to shared decision making is essential, given the operational circumstances and the characteristics of the organization. In these situations, the effective leader and decision maker will be the one who teaches others to lead themselves and take their own decisions.

Transactional and Transformational Leadership

Sashkin and Rosenbach (2000), in a review of leadership theory in which they identify major shifts, refer to Bernard Bass's work (1990) on transactional and transformational leadership. They establish the "old transactional, or managerial, side of leadership" as embracing subcategories such as

- Laissez-faire: abdication of responsibility and in fact demonstrating an absence of leadership.
- A system of reward and punishment, or "carrot and stick," that can be productive and satisfying.
- Management by exception, where managerial behavior is tuned to intervene to deal with problems or to handle situations when there is evidence of departures from procedures or deviant behavior. Some library managers might silently aver that this can be a full time job.

For transformational leadership, the authors describe a range of different behaviors:

- Charismatic leadership: the leader engenders excitement, pride, a sense of mission, and a vision.
- Inspirational behavior: leaders expect a great deal from their followers,

are able to present complicated ideas in a simple way, often using symbols, and can communicate a vision of the organization.

- Transformational leaders: capable of building good personal relationships, they encourage personal responsibility, learning, and development, and they demonstrate trust in others. In exchange, they earn the trust of their followers.
- Innovative thinkers: transformational leaders offer new thinking, and they encourage followers to challenge conventional ideas and traditional ways of doing things.

Leadership and Organizational Characteristics

The last few pages represent a fairly conventional view of leadership, arguably faithfully represented in most libraries of the 20th and early 21st centuries. What makes these ideas inadequate is the changing nature of modern information services. There are a number of characteristics that suggest the need for a different kind of leadership. These organizational characteristics can be summarized:

- Technologically driven and technically complicated
- Hybrid ——a mix of the traditional and the novel
- Complex, in that there are many variables and unknowns surrounding the organizations
- Increasingly personalized from a user point of view
- Specialized, yet with a need for multiple skills
- A growing need for new skills
- Complex structures
- Facing competition
- Unpredictable
- Reflecting a mix of traditions, training, ways of working, and priorities
- Increasingly based on collaboration and the development of cross-sectoral initiatives
- Entrepreneurial, in that there is a growing need for new ideas and innovative thinking
- Based on learning as the bedrock of growth
- Team based and decentralized

These features must influence the leadership style if the organization is to be effective. What this means is that relevant leadership styles in the context of contemporary libraries are different in kind from those that have traditionally been seen as part of the makeup of a good leader.

Partnerships

The idea of partnerships runs through the organizations under scrutiny in this book. Teamwork is based on partnerships, cross-sectoral relationships are based on partnerships, and most information services reflect some kind of partnership between librarians and information technology specialists, although these are often in embryo form.

In a more general sense, the relationship between leader and follower needs to be a partnership. This clearly raises a question mark against the idea that the charismatic leader has a role to play in modern library services.

Charismatic leadership also seems to present another difficulty in organizations where there is a need to innovate in the face of significant change, and specifically in situations where there is a need to take risks. The literature reflects a view that charismatic leadership might entail a greater possibility of failure, and this can be damaging where the appeal of the leader is based almost exclusively on self-belief and a talent for inspiring colleagues. This kind of appeal might appear to be irrational in the cold light of day.

Charismatic leaders are often seen as authoritarian, given to acting on impulse, neither interested in detail nor with a good grasp of it, and without the essential leader's felicity for self-criticism. They usually possess genuine certainty and have a desire to dominate.

Another charge sometimes leveled at charismatic leaders is that they are centralists and find it difficult to devolve power. The relevance of some of this argument, which is also contradictory in parts, depends on how change in 21st century libraries is viewed. If it is going to be

- Revolutionary
- Accompanied by less reliance on traditional organizational structures
- Marked by nontraditional forms of authority and communication

then the charismatic leader may well be a natural part of the scene. If change is viewed as evolutionary, this will not be the case. As modern organizations move away from the idea that authority is tied up with personalities, then charisma will become less important. It is also undemocratic: Heroic leaders set out to convince followers to do what *they* think needs to be done (Valenty and Feldman, 2000), and the question of organizational democracy has an important bearing on leadership styles. This argument has to be balanced by the recognition that there will still be a need for vision, but whether this particular gift really demands charisma is open to serious questioning.

There is a view that partnerships in leadership, and in organizations in general, actually need not rely on charisma. Partnerships imply equality, while traditional leaders, who are often charismatic, see the relationship between themselves and their followers as one between a major and a minor player. This is inevitable when the inspiration for leadership behavior comes from ideas about traditional authority and about the use of legal power.

From working in organizations that were conventionally structured and behaved in conventional ways, it is difficult for me to recall many situations when a proposal of the leader did not carry the day. Although these organizations were genuinely participative in terms of the degree of debate, and often consensual in the way they did business, the reasons for this were not difficult to understand: the traditional use of power, a traditional view of the role and position of the leader vis a vis the followers, and—perhaps most important—a measure of charismatic leadership. It was this latter characteristic that was perhaps the most significant. It often created the situation referred to earlier when people were persuaded to do things they would not normally have agreed to. In certain circumstances, this could be the worst possible basis for leadership behaviors, particularly in contemporary libraries.

By contrast, the appropriate management of hybrid libraries depends on creating a partnership of equals (Potter, Rosenbach, and Pittman, 2001), free of the deference that sometimes comes with the aura of leadership. This partnership is based on

- Empathy: all parties involved in the relationship need to be completely attuned to each other. There must be totally unambiguous communication and awareness of the emotions, motives, beliefs and viewpoints that lie behind behavior. All this must be free of personal likes and dislikes.
- Mutuality: followers not only identify with leaders—leaders identify with followers.
- A shared vision: visions do not belong to leaders, they belong to everybody, and everybody has a role to play and an input to make in articulating the vision. Nor are visions simply a picture of what an organization or a service will be like in five, 10, or 20 years time. Visions are also to do with values, with how the service will be conducted, how the organization will treat its staff and its clients, and about the quality of what will be offered. Visions should also be put together as a shared exercise. Although there is a tendency to regard the vision as stemming

from a big idea or some kind of advanced insight, in fact it comes from disciplined, analytical thinking. Creating the vision is a skill to be acquired.

- Listening to others, and doing it properly, which is another key skill.
- Clarity: the nature of the compact upon which leadership is based must be made obvious and unambiguous. Everyone has to know what the partnership sets out to achieve, how it will work, and what the results will be.
- Collaboration: the point has been made that bureaucracies are based on competition, and this is also a part of the makeup of conventional leaders. Collaboration is one of the keys to mutually beneficial relationships between leaders and followers. Neither compromising nor conceding, collaboration is about problem solving. It is about finding solutions and ways forward that meet the needs of all parties in the relationship.
- Integrity: the whole relationship is a question of honesty and trust.
- Learning: collaboration, clarity in communication, listening—even empathy and articulating a vision—are skills that can be learned, and should be part of the learning process in the organization.

Putnam (2000) proposed a similar idea in his dissection of social capital. By this he meant the idea that democracy in the wider society depends on relationships between citizens. Renshon (2000) wrote that leadership capital is

- Competence
- Integrity
- Character
- Ability
- Performance

Exploiting leadership capital calls for leaders who are with their followers, yet can moderate some of their ideas and add a new dimension to their thinking. Leadership under these circumstances is reflective in the sense that it disperses power and works with differences and disparities—key components of hybrid libraries. These are also leaders who make horizontal links rather than working through hierarchies, and can seek a common purpose.

Equally instructive are Renshon's examples of how leadership capital can be squandered through

- Lies

- Felony
- Favoritism
- Incompetence
- Errors that could and should have been avoided

This is a summary of the need for a moral dimension in leadership, and it is appropriate where there is diversity, clashes of interests, and uncertainty.

Before we finally leave the idea of the charismatic leader, it is worth noting some of the ideas supported by Drucker (2004). Recalling some of the most effective CEOs he had worked with, he indicated some of their key characteristics:

- Variety in their personalities, beliefs, attitudes, strengths and weaknesses.
- Knowledge of what needed to be done, and what it was right to do.
- A belief in widespread responsibility and ownership, and hence accountability.
- Making sure everyone knows who is responsible for what.
- Making sure that everyone who will be affected by a particular development is in the loop and fully shares in it.
- Reviewing progress.

This leads to an emphasis on the skills of decision making and communication. Behind this is a more concrete practical framework. This sets out the characteristics that not only help leaders turn plans into reality, but make certain that the reality remains just that, and that timely revisions can be made when weaknesses in courses of action become apparent. In the heavily theoretical and technological environment of the hybrid library, this is an invaluable knack. Drucker emphasizes the intrinsic self-development contribution of this form of leadership, as well as its relevance to the pursuit of organizational objectives.

Amabile and others (2004) also tend to discount the significance of charismatic leadership. In a wide-ranging review of leadership and creativity—identified earlier as a key component of 21st century libraries, they supported the argument that charismatic leadership was not particularly effective in high-performing teams. Rather, respondents to their survey put a premium on the hard, practical skills of consistent support. This support was emotional, in terms of resource provision and also in a measured approach to things like control:

- Regular monitoring, but with enough space given to teams to ensure an

appropriate degree of autonomy
- Championing the team and their work
- Inputting information, expertise, and ideas in practical ways
- Publicly championing success

What emerges is an essentially hard-edged leadership which is based on an engagement with the world of work rather than a concentration on the strategic, political, and policy-making aspects of leadership, important as these things are.

Visionary Leadership

Sashkin and Rosenbach (2000) advance the argument and add something else to this concept of appropriate leadership. They see leadership as a mix of behavior and attitude, and argue that charisma is not the wellspring of transformational leadership, but is a manifestation of the way that transformational leaders behave—the things they do. Taking these theories, and the work of others, Sashkin developed a template of visionary leadership which he saw as a combination of behavior and specific personal characteristics, and which he crucially believed could be learned in the same way as behavior can be changed:

- Clarity means the leader's ability not only to home in on key ideas, but also to focus the attention of others on these critical issues. It is a process of lending clear-sightedness to the abstract complexities that exist in modern organizations.
- Communication is the "process of active listening and giving and receiving feedback effectively" (Sashkin and Rosenbach, 2000).
- The consistency Sashkin refers to is two-dimensional. It means consistency between actions and words and the consistency of both over a period of time. This is modeling, and the result is the creation of trust.
- Showing respect and concern was Sashkin's fourth behavior. He means the ability to suspend emotional responses or critical judgment of what people do or how they behave. This is supported by a pattern of actions, both big and small, that demonstrate an attitude of caring for others. Sashkin uses the examples of working to ensure job security at one extreme, and knowing and using people's names at the other.
- Visionary leaders invite followers to take up challenges that test them, and to take responsibility. This is also an important part of motivation (see chapter 7). But creating opportunities in this fashion involves cre-

ating situations where risks can be taken in a manageable way. It means providing the resources, help, and support to maximize the chances of success and make the risk a minimal one.

To these behaviors, Sashkin added some characteristics he considered to be essential in modern leaders:

- Self-confidence was the first of these and, of vital importance, it can be learned, so it is not a trait. In its essentials, this is the belief of a leader that he or she can achieve results. It is also the ability to imbue the same confidence and belief in their own ability in followers. This aspect is actually the more important one. Good leaders imbue confidence in others when they do not necessarily feel it themselves.
- A thirst for power is fundamental, but it has to be used properly and channeled. In all organizations, but particularly in modern, technologically driven organizations, visions become reality and objectives are achieved by the concerted efforts of everybody. Leaders need power to harness and coordinate the talents and drive of followers. The organization is controlled by "the exercise of power and influence," and without power, it is that much harder to exert influence. The caveat is that good leaders seek power in order to give it away or share it.
- Cognitive power is the ability to analyze how "causal chains affect each other over relatively long periods of time and achieve desired outcomes" (Sashkin and Rosenbach, 2000). This is akin to creating a vision based not just on how the leader sees the future organization, but also on the ideas of followers. While leaders have a responsibility to develop their own long-term vision of the organization, this will fail unless followers, who work within a much shorter timescale, also have the cognitive power to build and refine their own vision of the organization.

Leaders as Cultural Engineers

The library of the 21st century is based on diverse cultures, and this is seen as a source of potential strength (see chapter 1). Even so, its vitality and effectiveness will still depend on forging these disparate elements into a coherent whole. A major task of leadership is therefore to fashion the organizational culture. Given all the differences likely to exist, there must still be an acceptance of shared values and beliefs. Some of the features of this culture are

- Commitment to quality
- Proactive ability to prosecute change and deal with external disturbance
- Acceptance of diversity
- Valuing the individual
- Empowerment
- Dedication to learning and development
- Collaborative effort
- Self-belief

It is easier to set out these characteristics than it is to create a culture that reflects them, but there are things a leader can do to fashion a culture:

- Provide people with a straightforward expression of what the organization is about, where it is going, and how it will behave as it gets there.
- Share these views with the entire organization, and encourage its members to make their own input into the aims, objectives, and the desirable behavior as these aims and objectives are achieved.
- Act things out. Modeling is a key leadership behavior. Leaders must embody the virtues they extol, and constantly demonstrate the values and the beliefs they want the organization to stand for.

Conclusions

Polly La Barre (2000) quoted the commanding officer of the USS *Benfold*:

> What the infidels don't understand—and they far outnumber the believers—is that innovative practices combined with true empowerment produce phenomenal results . . . listen aggressively . . . see the ship from the eyes of the crew.

Empowerment and the associated ideas discussed in this chapter amount to a statement in favor of what has come to be called the "democratic enterprise" (Gratton, 2004). This as yet largely unrealized ideal is, in Gratton's view, not only achievable but essential. Gratton considered most of the attempts to empower workers so far as merely trimming, and in this she sees the continuing power of the belief in the heroic, or charismatic, leader. She goes on to identify some trends that are particularly apposite for libraries:

- The influence of technology
- Changing relationships between organizations and their clients
- Operating in times of change
- The need for more flexibility than is found in the traditional forms
- The necessity of engaging the interests of staff, and ensuring their all-round development
- The straightforward but sometimes elusive characteristic of fairness
- The need to constantly discover and use new organizational energies

W. Edwards Deming (1986) commented on the key relationship between quality and participatory leadership, but this is only half of the equation. Leadership is a key function in hybrid libraries, but it is not enough to concentrate on the undoubted case for visionary leadership of the kind described in the foregoing pages. There is still a need for mastery of detail; the practical involvement commented on by Amabile (2004), Drucker (2004), and Sashkin and Rosenbach (2000); good planning skills; and some of the other aspects of transactional or managerial leadership. While the emphasis on visionary leadership as a means of dealing with situations that are unclear, fluid, and full of diversity and potential discord is correct, the discipline of the conventional practices of management are still called for. This in turn influences how managers approach some of the key roles and skills outlined in this chapter and the previous one.

To expand on the main idea of the previous paragraph, one of the more negative characteristics of library management, it seems to me, has been the lack of an antimanagement perspective, referred to in the introduction and in chapter 6. Gratton herself comments on the automatic acceptance of the "right to manage" present in the psyche of many managers. There has always been a sharp differential between managers and doers, and it is almost a reflex action to assume the need for more management whenever an innovative new service or development is mooted. The organization of electronic resources into separate divisions or units, with their own management structures, referred to in chapters 1 and 2, is a prime example. Apart from building some more rigidity into structures, this practice also sharpens the perception that there are fundamental divisions between managers and managed.

Auger and Palmer (2002) present an alternative view. They trace the growth, in mainstream management theory and practice, of the idea of managers who manage and also discharge a practical, professional role. This concept appears to be particularly relevant to knowledge industries and those other sectors that exhibit the characteristics discussed in this chapter.

This idea of the player manager, common in many sports, and the related idea of the leader as coach, has implications for the management of hybrid libraries, and these implications are examined in the next chapter.

Chapter 6

The Player Manager

The power of tradition acts as a mighty counterbalance to any hint of change in the management of modern organizations. Although there is movement afoot, it is slow, and one reason for it is the culture of managerialism in which we all grew up. Tradition can be a source of strength in a profession that is overwhelmingly practical, and in librarianship most of our traditions are rooted in professional practice, but when tradition leads to entrenched attitudes it can be a debilitating weakness. One problem here is the tendency of bureaucratic organizations to separate professional practice from management. The ability to continue to understand and play a role in work at a professional level should be a requisite condition of the way we order our business as managers. Unfortunately, we work in a system that miraculously transforms a professional librarian into a manager overnight, and does not make it easy to retain a significant professional involvement. By doing so, we lose something that is valuable. Once the move from a professional post to any kind of supervisory role is made, the nuts and bolts of the technical aspects of what is after all an essentially practical enterprise, are quickly dropped and rarely taken up again, even in an emergency.

The trick of moving effortlessly between strategic thinking and practical involvement has always been a valuable management tool. This flexibility is still the bedrock of many small information services, and it should inform the practice of management in the widest sense. Some of the best current examples of this are to be found in healthcare libraries in the UK, where structural changes led to amalgamations of providers and the creation of the new Strategic Health Authorities and the Primary Care Trusts. The merged libraries that came out of this reorganization often demonstrate the virtues and vices of the player manager syndrome that is the subject of this chapter. They often have no discernible hierarchy, with just a single identifiable manager, and characteristically have many fewer organizational levels than mainstream public and education libraries. What this means is that the same member of staff can embrace managerial roles at senior, middle, and operational levels, as well as contributing professional skills.

The culture of managerialism referred to here and in the previous chapter is in evidence in many forms. It is seen in the separation of strategy from implementation, in the gulf between the planners and the practitioners, and in the preservation of vertical organizational divisions.

There are also other characteristics. This book argues that structures are vital, and are second only in importance to the personality of the manager. This is because only structural change, which is fundamentally influenced by the manager's personality, can permit and support the other developments that are equally vital to modern management. However much library managers tinker with structures to produce flatter organizations, real flexibility comes from breaking down the vertical divisions, and this is much more than a matter of structure. It involves a change in roles, for managers and managed, and it requires a substantial behavior change.

One of the key differences between library management and the management of knowledge workers in other sectors, reflected in the literature, is to do with this question of managerialism. A number of commentators note the growth of an antimanagerialism culture in the financial sector, consultancy firms, professional services in general, areas of education, health, and a range of other corporations and institutions. This has led to the emergence of what Auger and Palmer (2002) call the player manager. By this they mean managers who can demonstrate a balance of management skills, professional skills, motivational leadership, an attention to detail, and the essential practical techniques of management. They see this antimanagerialism as a powerful antidote to the inertia of traditional systems, and it is something that is applicable to the operational conditions of contemporary libraries:

> In the New Economy, as more and more people became involved in knowledge work, the shortcomings of general management became more apparent. Handling the unexpected in innovative ways was the key to competitive advantage, and the interdependencies between good business decisions and creative production become obvious.
>
> (Auger and Palmer, 2002)

It is necessary to see "the whole equation by fully recognizing the increasingly interwoven nature of producing and managing." It also has to be said that Auger and Palmer (2002) are skeptical about the willingness and ability of senior management to support the idea of the player manager. They are also brutally frank about the pressures the role creates. Pointing unerringly to the real dangers of overload in some environments, and to the massive pressure of financial targets and other numbers, they testify to the potentially crippling burden on the player manager. This does not, of course, invalidate the concept. It should also be noted that library services are as yet relatively immune to many of these pressures. A stronger counterargument is that measures such as reducing the hierarchy, cutting bureaucracy, and developing a team structure with power and responsibility moved down to the lowest possible level will produce a reduction in the managerial burden. Geryts (1995) wrote of the transformation of a library organization through both top-down and bottom-up processes. Over a long periof of time, this produced the characteristics listed above. One of the benefits Geryts referred to was the need for fewer meetings. This alone represents a significant saving in time spent managing. I would also argue, from personal experience over a similar period of time, that decentralization, genuine empowerment, the virtual elimination of the hierarchy, and sensible automation, also make player management feasible. A problem here is that many library managers are neither willing nor able to support the important idea of real teams in practice—a concept that has been part of librarianship for a very long time, but which we have fudged:

> An alternative . . . is to extend the Player Manager concept to a model that involves all players in a team sharing the managing. This option twins the concept of empowerment with the much-posited ideas associated with network organizations.
>
> (Auger and Palmer, 2002)

Donkin (2001) sees the apotheosis of the player manager in prophetic, if not for some traditionalists, apocalyptic terms:

> Within the next twenty or thirty years we may well see the disappearance of conventional management and reporting structures, replaced by interdependent networks engaged in transactional relationships.

What does this sound like if it is not the fully wired library?

The Player Manager

There was a time when player managers were common in libraries. There were many small information services that were based on the concept, although the protagonists would probably not have recognized the label. Staffed sometimes by a lone professional and a small number of often part-time assistants, they were characterized by

- Agility and adaptability: Enabling the organization to change direction quickly.
- Flexibility: Working across a range of tasks—professional, managerial, technical, clerical—displaying versatility of thinking.
- Multitalented: Demonstrating a wide range of abilities.
- Multifaceted: Commanding a range of leadership, managerial, and professional roles.
- Talented in the technical execution of the key business of the organization, while also capable of managing (Auger and Palmer, 2002).
- Possessed of "technical ability, positive thinking, tactical acumen" (Auger and Palmer, 2002).

The reasons for the existence of this role in libraries are not difficult to see. In large swathes of the profession, economics made it a necessity. Even if such creatures as professional managers had been around, it would have been impossible to justify employing them, or to pay for them.

Size was another factor, with many libraries in both the academic and public sectors, and certainly in industrial or commercial settings, simply too small to justify full-time management. The ultimate player manager sometimes emerged from stories, possibly only slightly apocryphal, of the commercial or industrial information service comprised of one man (or, more likely, woman), with not even a dog in sight to keep him or her company, and a telephone directory.

The underdeveloped education and training milieu of the profession also contributed. Without a structure of professional training, no management training, and often an academic qualification in something else, it is easy to see how the idea of the talented amateur took hold. In many services, the concept of the part-time librarian whose real expertise and more important contribution to the organization lay elsewhere, led inevitably to the adoption of the role of the player manager. One of the best examples of this is that of the old-fashioned "bookman" who saw maintaining an involvement in the selection of resources as a key function. At least one of these was still around, to my certain knowledge, in the early 1990s, when both the technological revolution and the idea of the professional manager divorced from other considerations were in full swing. In colleges, librarians were often lecturers as well, and as late as the 1960s it was possible to find libraries in the education sector managed by a senior staff member of a mainstream academic department, perhaps the ultimate player manager or scholar-librarian. Or maybe in the context of the library he was the consummate talented amateur. It is undeniable that these figures exist today in small units, and that the profession is the better for it. The difference is that the balance of responsibilities is now heavily tilted towards the managerial aspects of the library rather than the academic interests.

As libraries became bigger and more complicated organizations, so they adopted management. Hierarchies, chain of command, line and staff management, very strong middle management with neither an input into the actual work nor, sometimes, a genuine contribution to make to strategy, were common. Organizations based on command and control management became the norm. Classical and scientific management theory exerted a grip which is still powerful today. Layers of supervisors, middle managers, and senior managers, with strict and formal communication and reporting lines, gradually came to represent the standard way of managing libraries. While this was happening, practical involvement in the professional delivery of services was sloughed off, and full-time management became the norm in all but small library services. The assumption of wider corporate responsibilities also accelerated this tendency. The development of the library manager as a figure with no direct or immediate professional responsibilities was assured. In an organization where it could be argued that most of the key decisions—those that had an immediate impact on users—were taken on a daily, ad hoc basis, on the hoof, at the point of contact with the user, this might not actually be the best way to manage.

At the same time, as Auger and Palmer (2002) point out, there was an accretion not only of power, but also status, manifested in many ways by managers. This development was something that institutionalized the differences between managers and managed, and created yet another organizational fissure.

This is not to say the position was totally hopeless. There has been a reference elsewhere to the concept of the Library-College in the USA.[1] Here, way back in the 1960s, there were attempts to create a genuinely distinctive, user-focused, innovative information service that promised a fertile seedbed for player management. Martell also wrote about the client-centered academic library (1983). Yet as institutions grew, managerialism reasserted itself.

Towards the end of the 20th century, commercial pressures on all kinds of information services increased and inevitably brought with them the adoption of many of the conventions, attitudes, and practices of the world of business. Much of this discipline was undoubtedly necessary, and most libraries have benefited from the improved planning, budgeting, performance standards, staff utilization, user orientation, and overall service quality that resulted. Nevertheless, the downside was yet another layer of managerial sediment, the growth of even more specialized staff management, and more vertical divisions in organizations where the idea of ownership was cemented into the fabric.

While management practice in other sectors has moved well beyond what has been outlined above, libraries have largely remained preserved in the managerial permafrost. Returning to my favorite obsession, for example, there is a great deal of lip service paid to teams without a full understanding of what this means. Total Quality Management has been embraced without the necessary structural, behavioral, and attitudinal changes that make it possible, and the relevance of Knowledge Management has been obscured as the central idea has been hijacked by ideologues. Over a period from 1990 to 2004, Pugh (1990, 1997, 2002, 2004) found little change in many aspects of library management in the UK, with a few notable exceptions.

Why We Need the Player Managers Back

This book has already listed, ad infinitum, the reasons why our organizations need to change. We are facing the need to create organizations where

- Technological change, while seen as a major influence, is creatively used as a real management tool, and one that supports structural and behavioral change
- The hybrid nature of the services creates a demand for specialism
- At the same time there is a demand for multiple skills
- Combinations of print and electronic media make disparate demands
- Change is unpredictable
- User behavior is more informed and educated than ever before
- Libraries are no longer the sole guardians of information
- Services are run by personnel from differing professions
- Staff are now better educated and trained than ever before
- There must be more willingness to accept responsibility

If we look across this spectrum of better educated staff and the general need to respond to rapid and broad-based change, then we see some parallels with the old player manager of the early days: showing the adaptability and multitalented skills of the all-rounder with the flexibility to think strategically and tactically, the application to apply themselves to functional professional roles, the ability to project positive thinking and to motivate.

There are many strands in management thinking that have come together with technological change in libraries in a way that advances the cause of the player manager. Changes in ideas about leadership, the development of thinking about empowerment and devolved organizations, innovative organizational structures, and the increasing acceptance of the significance of the human element as the most important resource in an organization—all are part of an attempt to manage complex organizations in times of complexity. The hybrid 21st century library is a typical case of this sort of organization in this type of environment. This is the justification for the player manager, arguably the most promising agency for organization development.

The organization that could emerge would be without hierarchies and without unnecessary and now artificial divisions between managers and managed. But it would be possessed of flexibility, new ideas about leadership, and a fresh approach to motivation. Perhaps it is appropriate to say that the coming age will be that of the hybrid player manager. This term has already been coined, to describe the emergence of this phenomenon in the public sector in the UK (Brock, Powell, and Hinings 1999). Brodsky also summed up the tendency:

> In the old days, middle managers provided us with the information we relied on to run the business but computers eliminated that function. . . . There's an important difference this time round however. The middle managers we used to have were strictly support people. They never dreamed of doing the jobs they were overseeing. In many cases they didn't know how. Our new middle managers are proficient in the work they supervise. If we're short handed, they can step in and cover for other workers and they often do. So they're better managers. They know what to expect. They don't make unreasonable demands of people and they don't accept lame excuses. They can get more out of a department because they have the respect of the people they work with.
>
> (Quoted in Auger and Palmer, 2002)

Here we have it: dual functions, breadth of vision, motivation, role models, technical competence, flexibility. Later, Brodsky comments on the fact that computers now provide much of the information that used to be gathered and passed on by middle managers. Player managers can fill the vacuum this creates and at the same time shift the balance of power and influence back towards staff who actually do the work.

Roles and Functions of the Player Manager

If the idea of the player manager is not new, then the role has certainly developed since the time when it was a common function in libraries. While there may be some aspects of the job that resemble a combination of task and relationship leadership skills, it is a concept that goes well beyond this. Perhaps its real significance is that it breathes life into the team structure that 21st century libraries will need to establish.

Sharing

The first idea to absorb is that there will not be just a single, lonely player manager. If libraries are really serious about often-used terms like empowerment, decentralization, flexibility, development, and others, the entire team will be made up of player managers (see chapter 7). They will all contribute different things, and their roles will vary, but the first prerequisite of player management is the ability to work within this particular culture. Raymond (1998) offers a useful metaphor for this culture in his description of the environment in which Linus Torvald developed Linux. He compared the conventional software development approach to a cathedral:

> I had been preaching the Unix gospel of small tools, rapid prototyping and evolutionary programming for years. But I also believed there was a certain critical complexity above which a more centralized, a priori approach was required. I believed that the most important software . . . needed to be built like cathedrals, carefully crafted by individual wizards or small bands of mages working in splendid isolation, with no beta to be released before its time.

What Raymond actually found was something quite different, that he likened to a bazaar:

> Torvald's style of development—release early and often, delegate everything you can, be open to the point of promiscuity—came as a surprise. No quiet, reverent cathedral-building here—rather the Linux community seemed to resemble a great babbling bazaar of differing agendas and approaches . . . out of which a coherent and stable system could seemingly emerge only by a succession of miracles.

In this bazaar can be seen a number of lessons that are appropriate to the player manager:

Experimenting—"Throw one away; you will anyhow."

Raymond, quoted above, took the view that the first solution to a problem is often not the best and, by extension, that any procedure, system, or course of action can be improved when it is done for the second and subsequent times. Each time an issue is worked through, then there is an increase in knowledge. Acceptance that libraries will operate in an environment where things might not always, or ever, be exactly right, is a good grounding for dealing with uncertainty and unpredictability. It is also likely that admitting error is often the first step toward arriving at an innovative solution to a problem, or the start of a significant improvement in the way things are done. From the player manager, there is a need for

- A willingness to experiment
- Constant evaluation and refining of the way things are done
- A readiness to accept error and learn from it
- Curiosity about how things work in a broad sense
- Dissatisfaction with the quality of services, however good they are

We might also find in this some support for the ideas canvassed earlier, that of overlapping responsibilities and allocating projects to more than one team.

Involving Users

This might well entail a seismic shift. The players are not confined to the library staff, and the player manager, as well as involving the entire team, will also involve the users. They also are stakeholders. Users show a growing awareness of the use of information sources, and an increasing competence in the use of electronic sources in particular. It is possible for them to demonstrate independent behavior in information acquisition. They are also more knowledgeable about, and increasingly able to articulate, their own rights when it comes to quality of service. A willingness to find ways of bringing users into the loop and developing a dynamic relationship with them will be important. The significance of this, in an environment where there will be less of a distinction between staff and users, is that as the barriers come down the potential input into problem solving and development issues gets larger, and the problem solving and development itself improves because of the contribution from a broader constituency. What the player manager needs is the self-confidence to accept this.

This also applies to the general concept of the player manager—one among a number of players with equally valid views and status. Where there is a number of player managers, or player coaches, we are likely to see the practical implementation of some of the ideas discussed in chapter 2: organizational redundancy, where people are given more power, information, and responsibility than they actually need to do their immediate jobs; duplication of work and responsibility; blurring of boundaries, so that responsibilities can be shared; more than one leader; multiple channels of communication.

Valuing People

Raymond's view (1998) that beta testers should be treated as the developer's most valuable resource can be borrowed for use in this context. Player managers need a heightened sense of the value of the human resources in the rest of the team. These human resources include the users. If the others, all player managers to a degree, have no sense of their own worth, self-managing teams will fail. If they are treated as if they are the most valuable resource, then that is what they will become.

Taking a Community View of the Organization

A team packed with player managers is a different kind of team. While a conventional approach to team composition and team building is a solid base, the idea of community needs to be prominent in the thinking. The bazaar Raymond wrote about (1998) is a confusing, vibrant, diverse, and colorful place. Without a powerful sense of unity or a strong sense of community, there will be no effective combination. This sense of belonging originates with the player manager, who has a strong role in developing the culture of sharing and responsibility. The power of the idea of player managers is partly derived from this source. The role bears the responsibility for building a culture that establishes values and sets out the way things are done.

Changing the Conditions of Work

The player manager's combination of managerial skills and competence as a professional should lead to a different way of managing. Some recent surveys by recruitment specialists in several countries indicate a widespread belief, in a range of organizations, that managers are ignorant of much of what goes on below their eye-line. Over 50 percent of employees believed that managers did not know what their workers did on a day-to-day basis, and that they were not aware of key operational issues. The same percentage of people believed that their job descriptions bore no relationship to what they actually did. This is a dangerous position to occupy in any case, both for managers and managed. It is doubly dangerous when there is volatility and rapid change. One way of dealing with it is to put the manager into the working situation, which is what the player manager does. The payoffs will be greater awareness of what others do, a better sense of well-being, stronger motivation, and more creativity.

Focussing on Performance

All managers focus on performance. The player managers' focus on performance is sharper. They will not only establish and maintain systems that have quality and performance ingrained in them, they will also develop the broad-based approach that is the flipside of W. Edwards Deming's view of Total Quality Management (1986), and will become the kind of managers that Deming had in mind when he wrote of

- Managers whose attitudes and actions will help people improve
- Managers who create complete transparency within the team
- Managers who do not set targets, nor deal in statistics
- Managers with a sweeping concept of communication
- Managers who believe in learning and development at all levels, including their own, and support it
- Managers who embody a commitment to quality
- Managers who lead without coercion
- Managers who intervene judiciously in professional processes and in service delivery

Demonstrating a Set of Values

Player managers operate in a stressful environment where there are contradictions, ambiguities, and often a tension between the two halves of the job. Coping with this depends on the strength of the player manager's belief in core values. Some of these are the values of the general management philosophy that underlies the idea: of commitment to sharing authority and power, openness in dealing with people, networking, collaboration, dialog. There will also be elements of a professional philosophy: the value of the mix of managerial and professional skills applied to working situations; a corresponding belief in the impact of this approach on motivation and teamwork; a commitment to quality in terms of organizational and individual benefit; the willingness to see organizational life as a learning experience and to ensure that everybody has that experience.

It is also to be hoped that the personal values of trust, honesty, personal and professional tolerance, and belief in the ability of the individual will play a part. Without the skill of communicating a sense of this solid ethical base, and embodying it, player management can degenerate into a desperate attempt to simply get the job done.

What is developing here is an extension of the view of leadership capital developed in the previous chapter. The idea of the player manager also embodies something of an ethical approach to management and organizations. This fits with the increasing significance of ethics in the profession.

The Dangers of the Player Manager

Autocracy

At the other extreme, the concept can lead to autocracy as player managers, involved in everything, attempt to personally drive the service forward through the power of legal or formal authority. The danger of this in an environment that calls for collaboration and teamwork is self-evident. The kinds of organizational values that could be demonstrated under an extreme version of the player manager regime would be counterproductive in the world described in this book. To start with, there would be no effective organizational learning. Ownership, that old bureaucratic idea that should be anathema in the digital/electronic/hybrid library service, would once again gather force. The associated vice of competition between individuals, sections, and departments would again flourish. All through the organizational spectrum, expectations of empowerment would be dashed.

Loss of Objectivity

Player managers are pulled in two directions. They move between two roles and attempt to balance conflicting demands. Without the ability to stand back, look dispassionately at the work situation, set their own personal priorities, and decide when to intervene in operational issues, the pressure increases. It is therefore important to retain a sense of balance and equity in allocating immediate priorities between one role and the other.

Managing in Too Much Detail

Working with too much detail can also be a problem. Managers in the more flexible and less structured team environment can sometimes take comfort from a misguided attempt to manage the micro-environment, and try to retain a grip on far too much detail. If the management part of the equation is to succeed, it will call for a broad-brush approach.

At the same time, player managers cannot neglect the playing element. They are still in the team and are still team players. One of the besetting problems of managerialism is the fact that managers accrue all the trappings of being above and outside the rest of the organization. The hierarchical organization lays down a natural progression from practicing at the lower levels to managing at the top, and compounds the issue by attaching benefits to management that are not enjoyed by other groups. There is a temptation on the part of the player manager to carry this over into the new environment. Striking the right balance between a number of elements and retaining sight of the team ethos, and indeed of the rest of the team members, is the way of avoiding this trap.

To state the obvious, the crucial interface is that between the role of player and the role of manager. The ideal context of the player manager is the self-organizing or self-managing team. This context will not spontaneously create itself (see chapter 7), but requires a formal and organized approach to organization design and development. It is a genuine and powerful mix of the essential hard-nosed practicalities and allowing people the freedom to do things their way, all directed at meeting concrete team and organizational objectives.

Player management must be a part of the organizational culture. It must be officially recognized, and it must be backed up by formal and informal learning systems. The player manager must also deploy a system that sets priorities, establishes guidelines, and underpins an across-the-board approach. Auger and Palmer (2002) refer to the use of 360-degree evaluation, leadership, personal effectiveness coaching, and communication skills as key devices to establish and sustain a balanced approach.

Within this balanced approach, there are a number of specific tasks:

- Taking significant responsibility, probably for the first time
- Continuing to model a standard of excellence in actually playing the game
- Sustaining a culture that supports change
- Developing a broad perspective

The Wider Perspective

Player managers start life as players. Presumably they develop a degree of expertise in the professional roles they discharge, and perhaps also some insight into a few of the technical aspects of management. What they will not do is acquire experience of organization development and specifically of team dynamics. They will also lack the political awareness, the broader institutional engagement, and quite possibly a knowledge of the external environment. While acquiring these skills is a matter of experience, this kind of growth is actually what teams are for. Within the culture of the team, an input from the other players is important. A properly constituted team will not only reflect a variety of roles, but also a variety of experience. It will in fact become a team of player managers, the sum of which will then provide the missing components.

This idea of multiple leadership is one that has attracted little attention in the literature of teams in information services. There are tried and tested models of this team structure, and the use of more than one leader has an impeccable pedigree. Pugh (2002) draws on models from military management. The metaphors already mentioned—of jazz bands, operas, and symphony orchestras have been used by other writers, as referred to in this text. Without this concept, the player manager would be placed under enormous stress, and would remain no more than an impossible ideal.

The Need to Know Everyone

Things coalesce around the player manager. Becoming the fulcrum of a team is demanding and brings its own problems. This is another area where a balanced approach is required. No team will be made up of equally strong performers, and there will be times when performance flags. There is a natural tendency for team leaders, whether player managers or not, to focus on working with the stronger players to the partial exclusion of the others. Team performance depends on all the members, and the player manager's key skills should embrace the ability to develop this even-handed approach (see chapter 7).

How to Create Player Managers

Every textbook ever written on change management contains the exhortation to develop a new management style. Some writers on change management argue that persuading senior management to unwind their tightly bound bureaucracies can be the biggest obstacle to organizational change.

If this is so, then the leap of imagination that is required to enable the executive to understand the vitality, the power, and the practicality of the idea of the player manager is enormous.

Player management is one of the things that benefits from a degree of top-down development. It has to be subscribed to by senior managers in the first instance, and it has then to be championed and sponsored until it is accepted by middle management. Following that, it has to be nurtured and helped to flourish. Although player management is at its most effective in middle management, it is also possible and desirable at senior management level, and it is here that the initial stimulus must occur.

Buying In to the Idea

It is manifestly clear that bureaucracies can be engines for successful innovators. There is also more than a suspicion that librarians might be more attuned to, and comfortable with, bureaucracies than with flat, organic structures. To espouse a system that empowers all staff, that encourages development, and makes the best use of all the talents available within the organization takes an act of belief. The logic behind this belief is that in the singular context of the 21st century library, bureaucracies will not be able to utilize all the available organizational talents with sufficient speed to deal with change.

The other basic argument is that the traditional approach to organizations puts too much dependence on management. This leads to a waste of human capital. Managers who remain in touch with professional issues, and continue to exert some of their technical skills, will be better managers. Other aspects of organizational life will also improve. Strategy and policy will benefit from an informed input from outside senior management. The all-round development of individuals will be quantitatively better from the experience of working on a broader canvas. Motivation will improve as jobs become more engaging. Players will begin to acquire the advantages of working in a political dimension—and in the end management will improve in this respect as well. The flexibility to respond quickly to change will also be increased. Organizations will become more fun, and in the pressurized orbit of modern information services, this benefit cannot be underestimated.

The idea of the player manager also has an impact on organizational creativity, a central theme in chapter 2. The player manager concept is a sure way of creatively harnessing the tension between the two roles of manager and worker. It is also a force to be used in making the best of the multifaceted and interlinked nature of information services.

Learning

In knowledge organizations the need for the manager to remain a player has been a common theme throughout this chapter. Organizational health clearly depends equally on the ability of the player to become a manager. This is a major learning exercise and demands the entire panoply of techniques, resources, and devices that can be pressed into service by the organization. It is likely that undertaking this will be the first concerted in-house attempt to introduce systematic, across-the-board management training, and that in itself will be a benefit. The learning system is one of the unifying threads in a team-based organization, and the concept, procedures, styles, and systems of the player manager will play an important part in organizational learning and the dissemination of the ideals of player management.

Changing the Structures and Building Teams

Teams are the obvious prerequisite of player management. The concept depends on a premeditated assault on structure, so that teams can be developed and integration can develop without impediment.

Yet some unifying devices must remain. The learning subsystem is one of these. The communication system must also be capable of handling all the information generated by the organization, enabling a dialog with other teams, and facilitating high level communication within teams. Relationships, dialog, learning opportunities—especially learning how to be a manager and to manage oneself—and the information loop that ensures all the players have unfettered access to all the information they need to do their jobs and fulfill their dual roles, will all contribute to providing a sense of direction. Here again, flattening the organization, dismantling the rigid framework, empowering individuals, encouraging the job enlargement and job enrichment that is the basis of player management, have to be replaced by something. The features discussed here will dictate a more subtle and organic form of direction setting.

Note

1. *The Library-College Journal* (New York, Library-College Associates 1968-) published quarterly for some years, is an invaluable source of information on an interesting and dynamic development in innovative library management in the mid to late 1960s and early 1970s.

Chapter 7

Motivation

Most of this book is in fact about motivation. In making the most of the characteristics of the hybrid library to create a stimulating work environment; in developing ideas about leadership, learning, and team structures that are appropriate in the hybrid libraries context; in considering issues to do with learning in organizations, the common purpose is to help people make the best of their jobs. However, the first difficulty in considering motivation in modern library services is ironically to be found in the very characteristics that make hybrid libraries a fruitful environment for organization development. Some of these characteristics make motivation harder.

Organizational Characteristics and Motivation

Incentives

Organizations that are already taking the issue of flat structures seriously will eventually face the need to confront the motivational implications of what they are doing. The ability to see a logical career progression is one of the factors that, in their early professional days at least, drives some librarians onward. The presence of a hierarchy, with the other features of the bureaucracy, offers a reasonably sure and predictable career path. When structures are flattened and organizational layers removed, then the path becomes less clear. One of the key motivational drives therefore becomes less intelligible in more flexible structures, where "onward and upward" can become onward and sideways.

Teamworking, one of the features of flatter organizations, also changes the dynamics of motivation in another way. Motivation is no longer a comparatively straightforward process of identifying individual goals and providing the necessary impetus for these to be achieved. It is also a matter of marrying these with team goals.

Higher Order Needs—Status and Power

Behind the goal setting lies the often unstated bureaucratic tradition of competition that has been referred to elsewhere in this text. Enhanced status or more power are acquired at the expense of another individual, or sometimes another department, and are obviously the result of competition. This in itself breeds unhelpful ideas about exclusivity and ownership of territory and ideas—concepts that are increasingly problematic in an environment where boundaries are coming down and where views on what constitutes expertise and a proper skills base are changing. There is another implication in that we also have to assess very different professional contributions to the work of information services. These increasingly come from nonlibrarians and raise the question of rewards.

The issue of status, a strong enough motivation for some, is inextricably tied up with the bureaucratic structure of conventional organizations. When hierarchies begin to disappear, then status, depending as it does on formal position and on the obvious symbols of position, becomes a problem. Still a powerful motivator in conventional organizations, formal status is less potent as a motivator in the collaborative, team-driven organization proposed here.

To most people working in conventional libraries, development involves movement up the structure. It also involves a move from practicing the professional skills, through tactical and operational management, to strategic management. In a world of collaboration across internal boundaries, between organizations, and within and between physically distributed teams, this kind of advancement should be less prevalent and less desirable. Our prevailing culture at the moment makes it difficult to accept that movement across an organization can be something worth aiming for and can legitimately represent development. It is also difficult to accept that status and authority do not necessarily come from formal position, so there is a large cultural shift to be made before we come to a realistic understanding of how to motivate ourselves and others in the virtual or hybrid library environment of the future.

Power and status are also components in the relationship between managers and managed. If accountability, authority, responsibility, problem solving, and responsibility are shared, and if flatter structures and stronger lateral communication, especially between the center and the distant workers on the periphery, provide easier access to management, then relationships become more equal in any case. In this more relaxed environment, motivation will be more sharply people-centered, and the need for increased provision of resources—including managerial time and learning—for supporting individuals will undoubtedly underline the significance of hygiene factors in motivating the workforce. A culture of empowerment will also be an important feature.

Rewards

A pertinent question raised by this discussion is that of how rewards are earned and delivered. Given the collision of librarians, computer experts, media staff, and others in present-day library services, this represents another obstacle. Implementing a proper reward system, while it is still an integral part of motivation, is not the straightforward process it seems to be in a bureaucracy. This is acutely felt where information services are based on conventional library, media, and IT services. Market conditions, reflecting a view of the differing marketability of library and IT skills, sometimes dictate attempts to introduce salary differentials. These might well be justifiable on market conditions alone, but could be problematic in team environments. It is noticeable that one of the models discussed in chapter 9 more often than not eschewed any significant salary differentials.

Some library services have found a way of dealing with this problem by tying rewards to the acquisition of new skills. These skills are particularly those that can be applied in other parts of the organization or that form a basis for job enrichment, job enlargement, and ultimately self-management. However, until the general issue of human resource management in virtual or distributed organizations is addressed, the question will continue to raise doubts about the efficacy of incentive theory as an explanation of motivation in modern libraries. In some environments, the growth of unionization may also have an impact on how this is resolved.

Equally important, the organizational model for the 21st century is based on power sharing and the inculcation of the habit of self-management for individuals and for teams. This weakens one of the key motivators—the acquisition of power.

This is another way in which the distributed teams proposed in chapters 8 and 9 offer an advantage. In this model, status does not depend on position, and there is no real hierarchy. Status stems from performance and the possession of skills. The same can be said of the exercise of power, which is again based on expertise and skills rather than organizational rank or title.

In the model, there are also multiple centers of power, close to the action, and literally so in some of the examples used.

There is also a commitment to multiple leadership. This requires the subjugation of the urge to seek the exclusive exercise of more control and the accrual of more and more territory. Where the boundaries are permeable and the team invisible in a sense that goes far beyond the impression of invisibility parts of the organization can already create for managers, ownership is a problem. In motivational terms, there is another adjustment to be made here.

Lastly, on this point, the reward systems in the examples used in chapter 9 are equable, and they do not value any one specialization or role above another.

Maslow's hierarchy of needs (1943) proposes status as one of the higher order needs, and places it, linked to self-esteem, at the apex of a triangle. In postmodern organizations there will be a requirement to reconfigure our thinking on what constitutes status and how self-esteem is measured in organizations where these characteristics are not tied to structures.

The Problems of Not Being Seen—Modeling

Managers should develop a talent for demonstrating, in their own behavior, the way they want others to behave. This is a powerful aid to motivation. Representing, on an everyday basis,

- A commitment to learning
- The skills of collaboration, power-sharing, partnerships, and operating across boundaries
- The proper use of communications protocols
- Empathy and listening skills

as well as acting out the practical leadership discussed in the last chapter, will still be important. The difficulty is that most of the skill of modeling depends on personal contact. With some team members working at a distance, some physically adjacent, and some working alone, this will obviously be uneven. There are no easy or complete answers to this, except for the development of a powerful culture that binds distributed workers together. This culture will include multiple leadership and, of vital importance, the correct use of communication. Given the reliance on electronic communication described in chapter 3, communication is a key function where managers removed from face-to-face contact can and should model desirable behaviors. Attention to developing an all-round pattern of social, professional, and personal communication in the use of e-mail messages and other forms of communication dealt with earlier in the book will help to set the tone and establish what is expected of all staff.

What Will Work?

Some of the conventional techniques of motivation are still relevant, as indicated above. There is also much that can be achieved by a shift of emphasis to embrace self-realization, self-development, and self-motivation. This can be done through enabling individuals to set their own targets. Self-criticism can also create it. What should not be forgotten is that teamwork, even in distributed teams, can also be a source of motivation.

Hygiene Factors

Herzberg (1959) put forward the view that there are features of the organizational environment that tend to act as positive stimuli to workers, and that there are other features that tend to reduce their enthusiasm and energy for what they do. A positive response to work depends on

- Participative strategy and policy formulation
- Structures that improve communication systems and support flexible attitudes to roles and responsibilities
- Empowered staff
- Transformational and inspirational leadership embracing coaching, mentoring, and modeling
- Learning
- Making work interesting

The most positive of Herzberg's findings was that work itself can be attractive and act as a motivator. The implications here are that jobs should be made interesting, should also involve collaboration, and should be demanding. This puts Expectancy Theory under the microscope.

Expectancy Theory

Put at its simplest, Expectancy Theory submits that

- The biggest demotivators are boredom, a failure to engage workers in what they are doing, and presenting people with unchallenging tasks.

If these features are present in a working situation, then workers are likely to underperform, and their skills and knowledge will be underutilized. The task then is to design jobs in ways that eliminate the boredom and set challenges. Making jobs sufficiently formidable and interesting is once again based on some mature ideas from the theory of organization development (OD).

It might also be beneficial to occasionally put staff into a position where they have to extend themselves and aim for an objective which might be slightly beyond their reach. The lessons to be drawn from overreaching, providing that people can be helped to cope with a comparative lack of success, and to learn from that experience, are valuable.

Long personal experience with overreaching and consequent under-achievement suggests that this situation requires careful management if it is to be used as a motivator. While attention to the hygiene factors in motivation will create the right environment, personality factors are also important, as McInerney and McInerney (1998) point out. This means that the leader has to make a fine judgment on the psychological capacity of individuals to tackle challenging tasks and learn to absorb the lessons.

Related to this, the motivation of individuals is influenced by the degree to which they expect and value success. For high-need achievers, success is more important than failure, while for low-need achievers, avoiding failure, which is not a good motivator, is more important than achieving success.

Whatever the psychological makeup of individuals, the prospect of success must be realistic. At the same time, there must be a challenge. This comes in the shape of objectives that cannot be attained without some form of personal or group development. Support in dealing with failure, and learning from it, must also be guaranteed. Objective setting and targeting for all staff is an essential element of human resource management and a powerful aid to motivation.

Organization Development (OD) methodologies make work interesting and engaging through

- Job enrichment: giving people responsibility for more aspects of the work they do, leading to self-management, as well as broadening horizons, setting stiffer challenges, and creating the need for skills enhancement.
- Job enlargement: combining jobs and merging responsibilities, to the same effect, and laying down some important characteristics of team-work.
- Team-based organizations.

OD also pays attention to the environmental conditions inside organizations. In the virtual environment, the socializing value of the organization
has less impact, communication patterns and procedures make it harder to
develop the rounded relationships that help meet emotional needs, and individuals may work in comparative isolation without the all-round support of
colleagues. Motivation will assume a different character. It is also a truism
that there will be concomitant changes in leadership styles and management behavior, including the involvement in objective setting, feedback,
and evaluation referred to earlier.

Along with the changes described here, there is also a connection
between Expectancy Theory, status, and the reward system. Hybrid
libraries, properly organized, present opportunities for learning, for growth,
and also for acquiring new skills. Given that the task is now interesting and
challenging and requires the worker to do much in the way of development,
then the reward must be seen to balance the effort put in. However the
reward system works, and it need not be exclusively through financial
gains, it must in the end make the job worthwhile. The benefits could in fact
be described in terms of the satisfaction of achieving higher standards,
enhanced status through the demonstration of professional skills, self-
development, and a greater sense of self-worth.

Self-Worth

This book is as much about change as it is about anything else. It is an
attempt to create a blueprint for organizations facing change brought about
by technological advances. The indispensable element in the situation is
how human resources are managed. Many features in the contemporary situation are novel, and organizational and environmental characteristics are
in a state of flux. The people at the core of this will increasingly suffer from
the uncertainty generated by significant and fast-paced change if the gurus
are right about what organizations will face. In these uncertain circumstances, their sense of self-worth, and their confidence in their own abilities, might be weak. The first objective of motivational techniques will be
to change this and foster a sense of self-realization in individuals.

One of Maslow's higher order needs (1943) was self-esteem, which can
be defined in brief as confidence in one's own ability and value. Pugh
(2001) proposed several stages that individuals could work through in order
to change their views of their own abilities. These were to

● Confront your own feelings: ruthlessly examine where you stand, and
  develop a balanced view of your capabilities.

- Consider other people's views of your performance.
- Look at your performance from the point of view of the organization.
- Set yourself some targets.
- Do something about achieving them.

The ultimate aim is to improve the self-belief of the individual. Cox (2002) says that this is done through learning and development, and is also a team activity. The systematic analysis described above is a part of this in that it leads to a realization of what has actually caused any success that has been achieved.

Intrinsic Motivation

The basis of the argument about motivation so far is that while some of the classical techniques are still relevant, the motivational significance of rewards, status, and conventional progression up through the layers of the organization needs to be reassessed. These issues will always be present, but flatter organizational structures are eventually going to reduce the opportunity for career development as it is known now. Changes in skills needs and the growth of a more heterogeneous work force drawn from disparate disciplines might present problems for the reward system and could require the application of a broader range of motivational ideas. Paradoxically, hygiene factors will become even more important in order to counter the difficulties of working in distributed and virtual environments.

There is also the problem that there is likely to be more flexibility and change in the work force, with increased use of fixed or short-term contracts tied to specific projects. The difficulty of using a conventional approach to motivation for staff who have no organizational future beyond the next two years is obvious, and as suggested earlier, the reduction in face-to-face contact is yet another difficulty to be overcome.

Motivation therefore becomes an internal matter and is less dependent on the actions of managers. Intrinsic motivation is applicable to teams, to permanent and temporary members of staff, to people working at a distance, and to those working in proximity to each other. It can also be practiced on and by individuals working solo, where motivation is often most difficult. McInerney and McInerney (1998) provide an instructive detailing of the development of theories of intrinsic motivation—motivation that centers on the self and draws its strength from the internal desires and feelings of the individual. It depends on

- A willingness to become involved in the job

- Curiosity about new experiences
- A wish to improve and excel at work
- A need to understand why things are done, to see a purpose, and set goals
- An appetite for solving problems
- A strong interest in work

(Andre, 1986; Heckhausen, 1991; Deci and Ryan, 1991; quoted in McInerney and McInerney, 1998).

The same authors also refer to evidence that intrinsic motivation is a more powerful force than extrinsic motivation in that it produces a greater degree of persistence and more flexible strategies for motivation. This is particularly seen in the motivation of distance learners, as one example.

Leaders and managers accepting the role of motivators therefore face the challenge of making the work interesting in itself and for its own sake—no easy undertaking in some areas of librarianship. Herzberg's hygiene factors (1959) also emphasize

- Participation
- Communication
- Empowerment
- Flexibility
- Learning
- Transformational leadership and collaborative management

Creating this kind of environment relies on the systematic organization development referred to earlier. The work must in the first instance represent a worthwhile challenge to the work force, involving tasks to which they can respond at their own level, but which will at all levels extend them and help them to develop. Even at the lowest level, job design has to incorporate this wherever possible.

In addition, an element of choice as to how people will work, and a measure of control that they can exercise themselves rather than work under supervision all the time, is also important in maintaining interest and motivating.

Simply inserting people into this working situation is insufficient without feedback from management, so this is the next element to put in place. It involves dialog and a participative managerial style. In distributed situations it also involves an imaginative but systematic use of the communications system to develop rounded relationships and real interaction on pro-

fessional, personal, and social levels. This interaction also has to be dupli-
cated across the organization, amongst peers. The practical steps to be
taken include

- Convincing people they can achieve in the new environment
- Designing jobs to permit development and learning
- Engaging in real and ongoing structural change
- Fostering cultural change
- Developing and selling a vision
- Giving people responsibility
- Communicating
- Changing managerial styles
- Dispensing with bureaucratic behavior

This all involves a combination of Expectancy Theory, Organization
Development, and Hygiene Theory. It lays a heavy burden on managers
and leaders who not only need to implement these changes but embrace
change themselves. This involves a revision of ideas about status, rewards,
and power, and it is a shared responsibility.

Motivation in practice involves two overlapping roles discharged by the
manager and the staff making up the organization. None of the steps to be
taking in creating a well-motivated work force belong exclusively to any
one group in the organization. Fig. 7.1 below sets this out as overlapping
areas, and sums up the main concerns of chapter 7.

Fig. 7.1 Roles and Responsibilities in Motivation

Part 3

A Solution

Chapter 8

Some Team Issues

The player manager of chapter 6 is the best option for the organization development that new-style libraries will need. The best environment in which this creature can flourish is the team. The indications are that there is considerable interest in ideas about teams and innovative structures and management styles, but that many libraries are still organized on the basis of traditional ideas and bear at least some of the marks of scientific management. This is widely seen in the structures and systems of information services: specialization; breaking all procedures down into component parts; an emphasis on the technology of library management—planning, budgeting, costing, centralized control; an emphasis on detailed measurement and assessment; the reserving of policy and strategy for senior management; conventional approaches to motivation and rewards; and the maintenance of vertical divisions in organizations. The emerging electronic services in libraries tend to reinforce each and every one of these characteristics. By extension, we are still perpetuating the machine model of the organization, albeit slightly modified.

The principles behind this model are still applied to the people who make the system work. The refinements that have been introduced into the management of resources in libraries are arguably still posited on the technological approach to management as described above. For example, no one can sensibly deny the need to know what library services are actually achieving, in the interests of efficiency, planning, development, and performance. We set targets for individual, departmental, divisional, and service performance. Yet most experts will also admit to the impossibility of fair and proper measurements of the performance of a library, and this is

why the less precise "performance indicators" have become synonymous
with performance measurement. However, far more important than the
methodologies, and the collection of statistics, are the key, user-focused
ideas of how good the library is at interacting with its external environment,
and whether it is capable of changing to meet the challenge of environmental change. Neither of these things can be measured on the basis of
inputs, throughputs, outputs, outcomes, cost measures, productivity, or cost
effectiveness.

It would be wrong to say that these indicators are not relevant to library
operations because they are. They are important politically, although their
operational significance is often less than is claimed. Gnarled long-term
observers might also suspect that on a day-to-day basis some library managers manage to conceal a healthy disrespect for measuring things. But the
issues of change and interaction are far more relevant to the assessment of
quality in a contemporary information service than the statistical approach
already outlined. The point being made here is that the latter approach is
part of an attitude that draws much from scientific management and is out
of synchronization with the sort of environment in which libraries now
work.

Equally, no sensible manager would question the basic validity of
understanding and meeting user requirements. Where the technological, or
managerial, approach can be challenged is on the grounds that it is almost
invariably a top-down exercise. Let us assume for the sake of argument,
and in spite of the sophistication of MIS this is a big assumption, that in
practice all libraries have the time and resources to collect the broad
swathes of information the technicians say we should. They then need the
time and the resources to make sense of it and apply it. Add to the mix the
jealously guarded roles of exclusive strategic planner, politician, and pub-
licist, to name but three. This amounts to a full-time concern for managers,
and the approach reinforces the conventional controlling and managerial
attitude.

This is part of an understandable attempt to eliminate uncertainty by
imposing a system when paradoxically the environment, internal and external, is full of creative and energy giving uncertainty and demands something else. To sum things up so far,

- Libraries are becoming distributed in terms of users and staff
- We are now capable of providing a service that is much more tailored
  to individual needs than before
- The work that goes on inside a library is also in some ways much more
  individualized

- The effort is now delivered by a workforce that is better trained and qualified, and more varied, than ever
- The environment is one of dynamic change
- As managers, we are less certain of the answers than ever before

Palmer (1998), while not necessarily subscribing wholeheartedly to the remedy proposed in this book, outlined a response:

> Dynamic environments require adaptive responses, sooner or later. The best way to achieve this is to distribute both knowledge and control to many business teams or nodes, rather than to hold them centrally. Hence the banner cry for self-managing teams, self-organizing teams and leaderless empowered teams.

Why Do Library Managers Have Problems with Teams?

Tradition

The answer of course is for the same reason that they sometimes try to measure everything that goes on inside a library service. For almost the entire history of organized library services, operations have proceeded in a reasonably secure environment, ignoring for a moment the burning down of various collections during political upheavals and the radical solution of bouts of sacking and pillaging in times of general turbulence. All our models and procedures, and our predominant organizational cultures, are based on the idea that we will continue to operate in stable circumstances.

This stricture no longer applies, but our organizational forms have not yet caught up because we still hold to the idea that organizations are about eliminating uncertainty. It is insecurity and a fear of the unknown that prevents us from dismantling bureaucracies and taking advantage of the creative power of uncertainty.

We are faced with a complex situation, in which there are many unknown factors. Teams represent an obvious response to the issue of how libraries should organize to handle the complexity that surrounds us. Unfortunately, teams also involve

- A different use of power within organizations
- The development of new roles, which will include a new concept of responsibility
- New internal boundaries

- Welcoming uncertainty

It is in the weight of our long and powerful bureaucratic inheritance that the difficulty lies when it comes to the necessary organizational changes.

Poor Models

Many library services assert the team-based nature of what they are doing. This leads to another difficulty in that it is often hard to discern much concrete evidence of practical teamwork. Most library teams are in fact groups (Pugh, 1990, 1997, 2002, 2004). They usually exhibit

- No element of selection—members of the group are often in situ when the group is established
- Some devolution of power, but normally no further than the leader
- Typically the presence of only one leader
- Some degree of interaction between group members, and some degree of mutual help and advice, but without any real dynamism that lifts the interaction to another level
- Jobs that are circumscribed and defined by rules and regulations
- A poorly developed learning function, including the crucial aspects of team behavior, individual relationships, team maintenance, and inter-team communication
- A lack of a cohesive program of general development
- Underdeveloped communication between groups

The result of the inadequate models we are using is that many of the groups in existence in libraries today are doing nothing to change the organization. There may be a degree of team development, but this exists within the rules of the bureaucracy, and the groups are part of traditional hierarchies and structures. The essence of the problem is that when we commit ourselves to team organizations, we put in place a badly understood structural change that should in fact take at least a year to plan, at least another year to implement, and would then be followed by a permanent period of growth. Geryts (1995), quoted in chapter 7, reported on a twenty-year development. Usually and conclusively there is in the end a comprehensive failure to consider the extent of learning and development that has to take place across the entire organization.

To add to this, there is a signal unwillingness to grasp the degree of personal development that individuals need to go through to make teams work. The problem is made more acute by the demands and conditions imposed by the development of distributed library services. These have been set in motion by electronic communication and other factors.

Player managers may be the best hope for managing libraries in the new millennium, but they need a sympathetic environment that can only be provided by a team structure. This may not be a conventional team structure because the teams referred to will be virtual teams for at least some of the time. Before we begin to look at this, we need to remind ourselves once more of the kind of environment in which these virtual teams work.

Virtual Organizations

Virtual organizations have actually existed in information services for many years, but for some time their presence went unnoticed. The view that virtual entities and distributed library services are things that have come about solely as a result of information and communications technology, and particularly digitization, is a particularly striking calumny. It is on the same scale as the idea that global organizations are phenomena of the late 20th and early 21st centuries. Morgan (1997), for example, traces these global players back to the 15th century city-state of Venice, which he suggests was an international financier of trade, and also notes the activities of the Hudson Bay Company and the Dutch East India Company, thriving by the end of the 17th century.

Similarly, there were many distributed information services long before they became networked: indeed they were probably in a majority well before digitization. The problems of managing, communicating with, and leading people who could not be seen are far from new. What is different is the emergence of information systems and information architecture that has revolutionized the scope and reach of distributed organizations. Multisite university library operations, the structures of practically every public library in the world, and merged organizations that led to administratively unified institutions operating with geographically separated centers, have been common for a very long time.

The standard managerial response in these circumstances was to apply large doses of bureaucracy in a vain attempt to retain control. It was also an attempt to overcome the psychological insecurity caused by managing individuals and parts of the organization whose key activities were in a managerial sense invisible. There is now an opportunity to change this approach through the development of ideas about communication, motivation, leadership, structures, and team building. This approach can be based upon a refinement and extension of traditional concepts of organizational design and development.

The key activities referred to above are to do with how a service is delivered on the ground in situations where the manager cannot see what is happening. One thing that managers hate above all is not knowing, and this feeling of ignorance breeds a lack of trust in the mind of the bureaucrat and a defensive notion to assert control. This writer, having once taken this attitude but now long outgrown it, is well qualified to comment.

Networks offered a means of changing this. The implementation of aspects of knowledge management theories, and in particular the increasing use of information systems as an organizational spine, make it theoretically feasible for people to work together across geographical divisions in a much more coordinated and accountable way than hitherto.

Other organizational changes are also relevant. The e-library has led to collaboration, alliances across sectors, commercial-public links, and the cross-cultural nature of some work groups in information services. More insidious and disruptive pressures often led to the loss of experience and knowledge as organizations shed long-serving members of staff. Doing so led to the disappearance of considerable resources of tacit knowledge that could not easily be replaced. All of these factors changed the nature of teamwork in virtual organizations or organizations with a mixture of conventional and virtual working. Much of the informal collaboration that goes on in work groups of all kinds, and in particular the exchange of tacit knowledge and the psychological support offered by these groups, is harder to reproduce in virtual environments.

Teams in the Hybrid Environment

Conventional teams, however incomplete their implementation in information services, all rely on a well-established body of theory. They should exhibit the following characteristics, in theory:

- Empowered individuals and work units
- Decisions taken close to the point where they are implemented
- A learning climate and individual development
- Job enrichment and job enlargement
- Streamlined and devolved management
- New processes for strategy formulation
- Improved communication
- Better environmental monitoring
- Integration across the organization, involving membership of more than one team
- A structure that maximizes all the available skills

- Multiple leadership
- Flexibility in terms of doing each other's jobs
- A degree of specialization
- An absence of hierarchy
- Rigorous selection of members
- Cultural unity coupled with differentiation
- A healthy degree of socialization
- A performance and quality orientation
- Powerful motivation
- Overall balance of roles, knowledge, and skills
- Awareness of how teams work
- A belief in teams
- Skills in dialog and collaboration
- A willingness to take risks

If teams are going to develop these characteristics and ensure that they thrive as teams and that the individual team members thrive, they need

- Personal contact (Handy, 1995)
- Knowledge of each other as professionals and as individuals
- Trust (Kimble, Li, and Barlow, 2000)
- Systems of informal collaboration
- Commitment and motivation

The basic characteristics of distributed teams remain the same as those relevant to traditional teamwork. The trouble starts because once teams become distributed, then the features that nurture these characteristics become diluted. It is obviously far more difficult to ensure effective personal contact where teams are distributed or virtual. Communication, the key element if team members are to know and trust each other, and to learn from each other, is a seriously awkward issue.

There are also additional characteristics, to do with team dynamics and management behavior, that have to be developed, and the turbulence surrounding these is exacerbated if there is an element of virtuality. Then the need for new forms of leadership, for some new systems of management, powerful communication systems, and new approaches to motivation becomes even more obvious.

What Kinds of Distributed Teams Exist?

The literature on this topic indicates that there are almost as many kinds of teams as there are managers. Three of the most common types are management teams, project teams, and process-based teams.

Management Teams

Management teams are usually permanent, and this type of distributed team is easier to set up, and run, than any other. There are far fewer difficulties in developing a team ethos at the top of the organization than at lower levels in the organization.

To a degree, it is obvious that management teams by their nature are naturally self-selecting—they are made up of the managers. This presents another conundrum. Some people would still agree that they should be solely comprised of senior managers. In fact, the case for this has become weaker and weaker in the face of devolution of power and the growth of the idea that perhaps other staff at other organizational levels had something to contribute to strategy and policy.

Without dismissing the opportunities for other staff to make an input into strategy, these avenues are rarely formalized and built into the system. The "grace and favor" and largely cosmetic offer of consultation is simply not strong enough. The additional difficulties inherent in establishing teams in distributed organizations make it axiomatic that membership of management teams should not be confined to managers alone.

Issues raised in the earlier discussion of player managers are equally applicable to management teams. They should reflect the balance of player management, and one way to do this is to include at least some of the player managers who are more concerned with playing and whose normal habitat might be in other teams.

Executive managers also have to become players. It should be noted that player management and distributed teams both demand devolved power, and devolved power does not mean simply shifting responsibility downwards. It also means figuratively shifting some of the personnel upwards. Representation from below on a management team increases the power of the team and adds another perspective. Conversely, it means that managers should be subject to the downward shift implied earlier, as they develop the roles of coaches and supporters in the professional arena and take up membership of other teams. Giving responsibility means taking responsibility for what happens in terms of professional performance.

Putting nonmanagers into management teams, in a way that means something and is more than a token, introduces differences. Teams are often thought of as a device for creating unity. This is true, but they are also excellent vehicles for harnessing the benefits of differences. By embracing different skills and specializations, differing points of views and backgrounds, and different professional cultures, they create the organizational energy that comes from multiple perspectives. This can only improve the health of the organization.

Teams also represent a secure environment for development. They provide a safety net for risk taking. They provide valuable reassurance in a more general sense, and this is particularly important in the peculiar circumstances of hybrid libraries and distributed teams. Essentially, they are mechanisms for capitalizing on the strengths of the individual members while allowing other members to compensate for the weaknesses.

Project Teams

Project teams are the second type of team. They may often be particularly suitable for the distributed environment. They are transient and fluid as they can be made up of members who sometimes join and leave teams for varying lengths of time, depending on the input required by the project. This may lead to the development of a pattern of working that is appropriate for distributed teams in most environments. They can cross departmental or divisional boundaries, work across organizational boundaries, and collaborate with other information services or external providers.

Process-Based Teams

Process-based teams are the most important kind of team in distributed library organizations. These teams will be responsible for the delivery of a complete package of information to users, and again could be working across organizational boundaries in order to meet all the information needs of a group of users. Some of their members will share a physical location while others may be working at a distance and relying on electronic means of communication. In multisite organizations, or collaborative structures embracing more than one institution, there could effectively be more than one team charged with similar or overlapping responsibilities, separated by distance but depending for their effectiveness on mutual reliance.

The Problems of Distributed Teams

Distributed teams represent a major opportunity for organization development. They also present the manager with considerable problems. The general conundrum faced by all of these teams is how to build effective cells without the essential physical proximity. Most, if not all, of our mod-

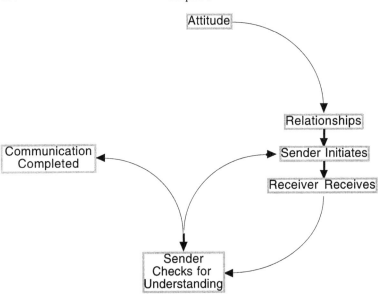

Fig. 8.1 A Conventional Communications Process

els attempt to deal with this. Communication is the key.

Communication

    Distributed teams miss out on all the nuances of subtle communication, particularly because the nonverbal aspects of communication are not available to all the members. The restrictions on the use of multiple channels of communication have a debilitating impact on the effectiveness of the process, and the absence of face-to-face communication is critical. This has a potentially devastating consequence for team dynamics. It can lead to factions and the isolation of some individuals and subgroups in the team. If we look at a simple presentation of the communication process, as shown in fig. 8.1, the difficulties will become obvious.

    Effective communication is a long-term process. It starts before a message is sent, and in teams it relies on the proximity of the sender and the recipient. Whether library services are distributed or not, we all spend insufficient time on developing communication in organizations. There is a tendency to regard it as a natural activity, but it is not wholly so and calls for conscious planning, preparation, and concentration.

Electronic communications, which may have to be relied upon to a great extent for distributed teams, in some ways undermine the basic communication process. There have been many expressions of dismay about the absence of a recall button for e-mail, for example, and it is likely that electronic communications have a demonstrable capacity to vitiate considered thinking and review. The sheer immediacy of e-mail seems to invite an off-the-cuff response. This may not be disastrous in a conventional organization where there are other methods of communication that can compensate, but in the distributed environment of electronic communication it may be all there is for long periods, and it can undermine team development.

It is also possible that there will be a two-tier communication system. Staff working in the same physical space can enjoy the benefits of a comprehensive communication strategy. Others will rely on electronic communication that might be less than comprehensive and less efficient. The need for a careful approach, and a considered view of strategy and process, is obvious if the introduction of another barrier to team effectiveness is to be avoided.

Communication is a matter of relationships. Its roots lie in the past, in a knowledge of the history of the organization, in the organizational background, and in the culture. These are the things that partly explain some of the relationships on which communication is based. Understanding these sheds some light on why people communicate with each other in different ways, how they do it, their style, and even what they say and to whom they say it. Acquiring this background knowledge in the case of a distributed team that might involve a completely separate organization is not easy.

Personally knowing the people involved, and cultivating relationships with them, is also critical—and equally difficult—in distributed teams. All forms of official communication are made easier if they can be tempered by social and personal communication, and comfortable working relationships grow if they are fed by simply knowing the characters involved on a personal level.

The lack of proximity rules out the use of physical and verbal clues, and in a way electronic communication tends to be less of a two-way process. True dialog then becomes even more difficult and adds to the problems to be overcome before any significant communication actually takes place.

E-mail itself is part of the difficulty. Often regarded within organizations as a purely business communication, it dispenses with most of the niceties of face-to-face communication and becomes a spare, focused, and business-only form of talking to other people. Many people consider it inappropriate to use e-mail in any kind of social dimension in work or even to use the common courtesies of memo or letter writing. The countervailing position is that if electronic communication is all there is for most of the time, then a slightly more imaginative use of it will pay dividends: Take time in an e-mail to talk about the weather, about other nonwork activities that are going on, to exchange social pleasantries. Use it as a substitute for face-to-face communication by building in some of the characteristics of the latter. There is a chance then that both parties will find out a little more about each other, feel more comfortable while communicating with each other, and start to develop a more rounded relationship. This will ameliorate some of the negative aspects caused by the sparsity of face-to-face communication.

Culture

Organizational culture has often been described as "the way we do things around here" (Glass, 1996, for example). The term covers a huge range of concepts like ideologies, relationships, service quality, the way that power is exercised, leadership, the mission and the organizational vision, myths and stories about the organization, communication systems, characters and personalities.

Culture can also be reflected in structures, for bureaucracies and organic structures stem from, and support, different norms. Culture involves the development of a set of ideas that can be shared and subscribed to by everybody. In practice, it offers a common approach that guides the way things are done and the way the organization and the personnel behave: a tough enough task in a traditional organization, doubly so in a distributed one.

An important issue that impinges on the establishment of an appropriate culture for virtual teams is that of trust. Creating this is a major task in the building of conventional teams. In virtual teams the problem is yet more acute because of the distributed nature of the activity, but also because trust is based on collaboration. The willingness to share rather than compete is not a phenomenon that occurs naturally in traditional organizations. Creating trust between the members of virtual teams drawn from more than one organization where rivalry might have existed previously, and where conventional team-building processes are invalid or less effective, is an even bigger problem. This is where little things like a more relaxed e-mail protocol might help.

Culture is also a means of creating a sense of identity. There are potential clashes here because team members in virtual teams can feel a sense of multiple allegiance—to their parent organization, to the team rather than the organization, and to the boundary-spanning team and project objectives. The trust issue, and the fragmented sense of identity, can both hamper the drive to share information. They can particularly damage the readiness to share informal knowledge.

Many elements go into the making of a culture, but one of the critical factors is the cohesive sense of unity that comes from close professional contact. This is one of the aspects that leads to a shared outlook and an agreed way of doing things. Where there is physical separation there is the possibility that there will be at least two cultures that might not share much common ground.

Underlying all of this is the issue of the mind-set. In information services our conception of teams is often not developed to any great degree. We have not yet fully absorbed the lessons of teams in other knowledge-based sectors, nor have we always accepted the relevance of team practices in some sectors of the creative industries. While we can acknowledge the intellectual arguments for team-based organizations, we are less good at turning the ideas into reality. To expect managers and managed to accept another significant shift and successfully move these ideas into the virtual environment means a major change in attitude and a new culture. This is a culture which supports a number of ideas:

- Teams can operate in a fluid, virtual reality environment
- Diverse environments add dynamism to the interaction both within and between teams
- Learning becomes even more important: By this is meant learning
  - About managing virtual teams
  - To realign the dynamics of teams to reflect the new environment
  - New perspectives on team roles and team composition
  - To live with uncertainty
  - New approaches to management
- There must be a reaffirmation of communication

The culture is the place, as always, where everything starts. While it is important to stress the new elements in the virtual team situation, and the need to adapt strategies and tactics to fit, the more conventional team-building process should not be forgotten. In virtual teams, there will still be a need to pay attention to developing a basic understanding of how teams work, how they are put together, and how relationships work inside the structure. Some of the work of virtual teams will still take place in the conventional arena.

Teams are a key part in the development of any culture, especially where there is a need for cultural change, as in hybrid information services. Laying down this culture is the first step in creating virtual teams. Most authorities would agree that cultural change comes about through

- Devolution of power and responsibility
- Changes in managerial behavior and attitudes
- Structural change
- Organizational learning

Cultural engineering in organizations is something that starts with leadership and management attitude, where the cultural sediment is laid down. Once again, distance and diversity present problems for this process. Case study 2 demonstrates the difficulty of forging a common culture in a virtual team spread across three organizations. Cultural change depends greatly on influence, relationships, and learning. Without the advantage of immediacy, this becomes yet another obstacle. It also has an affect on the quality of service because of the difficulty in establishing common standards across more than one organization.

Psychological Problems

Team processes begin to fracture when the members are geographically separated. It is difficult for teams to develop a sense of unity when the big picture of team activities is not apparent to all the members, where it is harder to develop the rounded relationships, the broad experience of working together, and the social and professional interaction that is available to the conventional team. Virtual meetings also lose some of the energy that comes from physically grounded team meetings and other activities such as brainstorming and problem solving, as well as team learning activities.

This sense of dislocation can develop into feelings of uncertainty, and often inadequacy, because of a lack of knowledge about what other members of the team are doing—how much progress they are making in their areas of special responsibility and how much information that might be useful to other team members is being missed because of communications problems. It is very easy for team members to lose their bearings if they cannot see how well their work relates to the overall picture or how it relates to the preoccupations of other individuals or other teams. This feeling of being out of touch and context can again be exacerbated by the differences in communication patterns between virtual and conventional teams.

The preferred channel for most virtual or distributed teams will be e-mail. This can be subject to delays unless there is an agreed protocol and timetable for dealing with messages. On another, more problematic level, the messages can be misunderstood or create uncertainty. This is because it is not easy to assess the emotional content, for example, in deciding how seriously some of the comments should be taken.

Some individuals will also succumb to a tendency to overcompensate. This happens in conventional teams as well, but in a distributed team communicating electronically, it can be a chronic problem. Communication becomes indiscriminate, excessively detailed, and almost a mindless reflex action.

At the other extreme, it can fail completely. Without a system for managing communication, including schedules, specification of what is to be included, the level of communication required for various activities, and even the style to be adopted, team effectiveness will be impaired.

The Information System

To prosper in the hybrid habitat, organizations need to divest themselves of features like layers, vertical integration, prescriptive job descriptions, careful and precise delineations of responsibility, and bureaucratic leadership. If they do this, they need to find some substitutes which provide a framework for normal working while still supporting creativity in the apparent absence of control systems. Knowledge management, and some of the other theories outlined in chapter 2, presuppose the imaginative use of the information system as one way of providing some reassurance, guidance, and a sense of direction in a more fluid environment.

Ironically, in a distributed context this can become a problem. The crucial aspect of tacit knowledge, as defined by Allee (2002), can only be effectively shared through personal interaction. There is no way of formalizing or institutionalizing the knowledge people never put on the record but carry around with them in their heads.

Tacit knowledge also takes the form of attitudes, feelings, the ability to reason, and innate intelligence. None of these can be logged as yet, but they are the very qualities that need to be incubated and maintained in modern organizations. Their development depends partly on how well they are communicated, and tacit knowledge in the sense of feelings, attitudes, and even intuition and insights, can really only be passed on through a human exchange.

It follows that there is much in the way of tacit knowledge that is learned from social intercourse with others. This is particularly true of organizations where the personnel are drawn from different professional groups and there are multiple perspectives on what should be done and how it should be accomplished. There is a clear difficulty in supporting this kind of exchange in an organization where the informal communication system and the social system cannot be effectively extended across distributed locations or is only spasmodically available to everyone. While the information system forms the backbone of the virtual organization and virtual teams, it has its limitations, seen most obviously in its inadequacy in supporting the growth and utilization of tacit information.

Technical Difficulties

Virtual teams in distributed library organizations possess a number of advantages when set alongside virtual teams in the business world. For the time being, information services will be working mostly, but not in all cases, on only one timescale. Working across national boundaries, with all the added cultural issues, is not a significant issue at present compared to the world of global business. Kimble, Li, and Barlow (2000) sum up the technological problems:

- Lack of sufficiently well-developed telecommunications
- Cost implications
- Technology that is designed for a conventional office and is therefore inappropriate for distributed working
- A residue of mistrust of the technology

The Solution to Creating Virtual Teams

The list of problems to be overcome in developing virtual teams is an impressive one. The answers lie in cultivating an approach that makes the best of what we already have while utilizing new technology and some new ideas about collaboration in organizations. This means applying the key techniques of conventional team development, that is, putting in place a logical process of team building. It also means making the best use of the technology available. Both of these actions need to be linked with ways of increasing the degree of informal sharing between virtual teams. Finally, and most importantly, it means that we need to change the way that we think of teams. This embraces thinking in terms of new metaphors and developing new models for teams in information services.

Building the Virtual Team: The Process

If we are working in an environment where it is seen to be necessary to

[push] responsibility and accountability down deeper into the organization . . . break down geographical, functional, and cultural barriers, and enable people to think and act entrepreneurially . . . build an organization flexible enough to exploit the idiosyncratic knowledge and unique skills of each individual employee.

(Ghoshal and Bartlett, 1998)

then there is a clear need for a new organizational structure. There have been many attempts in the business world to recapture the advantages of the small business:

- Able to change direction quickly
- With workers who can contribute to a multitasking environment
- Able to focus multiple skills and talents on key areas
- Bringing all the relevant talents, from all parts of the organization, to bear on strategy, policy, and operations

If the player manager is the role model for behavior in this organization, then the environment, the culture, and the structure rely on the team.

There are some management principles that are immutable in the face of technological change of all kinds. There was at least an intellectual acceptance of the relevance of teams, flatter structures, new power centers, devolved decision making, the importance of a portfolio of skills, and other features of modern organizations well before the Information and Communications Technology revolution made a significant impact on information services. Basic organizations, in Mintzberg's sense (1979), being small, were ideal for changing direction quickly. Communication was straightforward and effective precisely because organizations were small. The smallness also meant greater equality all round, and so peer and team influence could flourish without hindrance.

The size of the establishment was also a factor in leading to interchangeability of skills and roles. Motivation was easier because the resulting environment lent itself to shared aims and objectives, and a common vision was often born out of adversity brought on by lack of resources. These organizations were in many respects more efficient teams than some today—there is little that is new in management, the Internet or World Wide Web notwithstanding.

One of the dilemmas for today, and this *is* partly due to technological change, is the organizational need to be both big and small at the same time, as a number of writers have pointed out. Latter-day developments in communication, together with emerging models of collaboration, and other aspects of postmodern organizations, merely serve to force into the spotlight things like teams and changes in management styles. They also underscore the need for total commitment to the basic principles of team building.

Many of the team characteristics listed earlier in this chapter are actually strengthened through working in virtual or hybrid organizations. Opportunities for learning and for job enlargement and job enrichment are greater. Technology permits the development of more powerful communication systems, and the frailty of the tangible, genuine hierarchy facilitates many things, not least a more powerful form of collaboration and better communication.

On the other hand, some more ethereal characteristics of teams are much harder to put into practice in the virtual environment. Motivation, team cohesion, cultural inclusivity, the development of dialog—all are much more difficult to achieve. Performance and quality issues across organizational boundaries are also problematic. These are issues that can make or break a team, and it is here that a return to basics is profitable.

The textbook approach to team building was laid down by Tuckman (1965) and has largely become accepted wisdom. The four stages of development established by him, and examined further by Bryson (1999) and Huczynski and Buchanan (2001) among others, are forming, storming, norming and performing. This reflects a process in which team members develop understanding of their own roles and the way these interlock with the roles of others in the team. They begin to establish objectives and commitment, a process of learning is set in train, and mutual reliance and trust start to emerge. A team leader is responsible for guidance, helps solve problems, and moderates in conflict situations. Eventually the team itself begins to take the lead while the original manager continues to function in a facilitating role. This approach was complemented by Belbin's work on team roles (1981, 1993) and in particular his views on the nature of a balanced team.

Virtual teams impose strains of a totally different order. In any case, the theory indicates a neat and tidy progression through the four phases of forming, storming, norming, and performing. Practical experience by contrast suggests that without a degree of care that is often missing, this careful and logical development can be impaired by unreconstructed sinners, recidivists, and backsliders, as well as driven forward by committed and imaginative teamwork from others. In other words, teams in practice are a messy, untidy, and complicated piece of substantial organizational development. If the task of creating teams in a conventional environment is difficult, how much more difficult can it be in an environment where

- Members are physically separated
- The geographical distance might be matched by cultural differences stemming from the disparities between two different organizational views of the world of work
- Motivational problems will be of a different order in the absence of face-to-face communication
- Proper communication itself might be problematic

The only solution to this is to rework the team-construction process and create a process that will provide a better fit with the requirements dictated by the distributed environment.

Team Selection

Most teams in information services are thrown together by accident. A group of people working in the same area by chance cannot be turned into teams without a great deal of luck, yet this is often the start of the process. Nor are they turned into teams if they are then left to the tender mercies of the same bureaucratic manager that looked after them before they became a team. The process of

- Establishing objectives
- Deciding on the skills and knowledge mixes
- Selecting the team members
- Implanting and nurturing a learning process to cover team dynamics, communication, team learning, self development, self-management, leadership, and other issues

has to be deliberate, systematic, and sustained. If the entire organization is to become team based, then selection is itself a long-term, organization-wide process of

- Matching resources to needs
- Counseling
- Training

Continuing Development

No team can be left alone, least of all a virtual team. Whatever the organizational structure, there will be individuals who once performed but have ceased to do so, some who never met expectations at all, and others who exceeded expectations. People will need replacing for various reasons, skills needs will change, and organizational needs likewise. Technological advances, and developments in our capacity to work with these, will make communication easier. If organizational learning is effectively pursued, aspirations will increase and capabilities will mushroom. Permanent attention to learning, to team dynamics and the mechanics of team behavior and relationships, will form key components in ensuring the continued health and effectiveness of the team, and these areas should also be part of a shared responsibility. There are also other, more immediate possibilities.

Control and Management

Are virtual or distributed teams amenable to the same forms of direction as conventional teams? The answer is probably no, for two reasons. The first one is that physical separation creates an increased possibility of aberrant behavior. Until the idea of open, multidirectional communication becomes a completely integrated, natural, and instinctive part of the team, there is a continued danger of fragmentation and discord.

The second reason has already been discussed. Virtual teams present a psychological problem for managers, many of whom still feel that what they cannot see or do not know about cannot be managed without difficulty. There is therefore a development issue for all virtual teams and leaders of virtual teams. As part of the ongoing team-learning process, there are areas that can be cultivated to deal with this.

Sophisticated and robust communication systems, and an equally important belief in the operational, cultural, and political importance of both the communication and learning systems, is axiomatic. As far as leaders are concerned, one of the best ways of overcoming the psychological problem of leading at a distance is to develop a greater understanding of the actual work processes of the team. Add this to the leader's portfolio of knowledge of team dynamics, the team members, communication, the political context, and his or her own expert contribution to specific work areas, and we are back with the idea of the player manager—almost a tried and tested way of dealing with the management of virtual teams.

In this way, control becomes a cultural issue. In a sharing, collaborative, less competitive environment where exploring, questioning, and dialog are given more prominence, the culture itself becomes a controlling factor. Relationships, behavior, and attitudes will create the discipline.

The outline of the culture sketched out earlier in this chapter contained references to

- Trust
- Self-management
- Openness in communication
- Identity
- Professional exchange
- Learning

with teams not only proposed as the best way of managing in a distributed situation, but also as a means of creating the culture. The elements in this list that have not yet been discussed are those of self-management and the professional exchange. Before moving on to these issues, it has to be stressed that self-management and effective professional exchanges, as well as team learning in general, are based on team cohesion. This depends on the ability to work together, and the ability to respect, and maybe even like each other.

In order to achieve maximum results, team members need to enjoy working collaboratively in general and also specifically enjoy working with the other individuals in the team. Part of this comes from knowing each other's jobs, which engenders some respect. There must also be an essential inclusivity that disallows the development of factions and promotes tolerance in an atmosphere accepting of objective criticism. Both the examples given in the next chapter, that of the bomber crew and the Red Arrows aerobatics team, demonstrate these characteristics to the full.

Self-Management

There are environmental and psychological differences between conventional teams and virtual or distributed teams, and common sense indicates that when there is an emphasis on collaboration across boundaries, then management styles and procedures must change to take account of this. The crucial emphasis is on the development of interactive styles that make use of the characteristics of distributed or virtual teams in imaginative ways that ameliorate the environmental and psychological problems.

Self-management is a logical extension of the ideas behind the concept of the player manager, and it is irresistible in a situation where the influence of the leader or manager might not always be directly felt. However, it is first necessary for managers themselves to change their styles. Earlier in this chapter there was a reference to the psychological problems of managing at a distance, and the first requirement is for managers to accept this and learn to live with it. Letting go is the hardest part of devolved management styles, and it can only be achieved through an investment in learning and communication systems. Learning is also the key to self-management.

Learning in Distributed Teams: Communities of Practice

Many years ago, the idea of the Invisible College had considerable currency. This was the concept of a worldwide network of scholars, academics, and researchers who interacted with each other using the channels available at the time. Totally uncoordinated, with no leaders and no structure, the concept expressed the practice of a nonhierarchical and protocolfree informal communication between experts. The members exchanged ideas and news and provided mutual support. It was all done through letters, conferences, published and unpublished papers, and face-to-face communication. In this phenomenon can be seen one of the early manifestations of the contemporary idea of communities of practice. Verspagen and Werker (2003) describe the invisible college as a congregation of research workers cooperating over geographical distance. The basis of this communication is an "informal narrative" based on a social network that supports a structure of research networks. This network provides access to important knowledge and information, develops relationships, and, of some importance, helps establish behavioral norms and beliefs. We are also today seeing a much more serious development of networks of scientists electronically linked and sharing knowledge and information in ways that threaten to bypass libraries completely. This is one example that underlines the need to manage contemporary libraries in a different way.

Although communities of practice are not in themselves teams, the principles can add something to our understanding of how teams might work in distributed organizations. The difference between communities of practice and teams is mainly that teams will usually have a much sharper focus, with clearer objectives and a stronger definition of purpose. What communities of practice bring to the discussion at this point is first that there is a way around the problems of building trust, overcoming cultural barriers, and dealing with the social issues of distributed teams. They might also shed some light on how to deal with the psychological problems of managing virtual teams or any other distributed part of the organization. Their procedures can be instruments for the creation of a varied and rich team culture, and as they are based on establishing behavioral boundaries, they can contribute to team management. They can also support the participative elements of teamwork and are learning mechanisms.

The definitions of communities of practice have broadened, as Kimble and others (2000) pointed out, so that they are now applied to groups and teams of various hues. What they appear to have in common with teams, and with some of the theories set out in chapter 2, are features like shared projects, problem-solving activities, exchange of experience, and learning. What is also interesting, but not unexpected, is the pattern of communications between teams, which appears to depend on membership of multiple teams, as suggested in the model (see chapter 9).

Over time, the performance of members changes, and some naturally reach the end of their time as team members by virtue of job or role changes, changes in team objectives, or other more violent departures. Knowing when to change the composition of a team is an issue in most areas where teams are used, and in virtual teams this is related to difficulties in performance assessment. One striking feature of the activities of communities of practice is the use of what Lave and Wenger (1991) called "Legitimate Peripheral Participation," or LPP. Translated into team dynamics, this means the absorption into the team of what might be called apprentices who play a peripheral role in team affairs while they absorb the culture, develop the trust, share the knowledge, and learn the procedural aspects of virtual teamwork. Ironically, this is simpler to achieve in a virtual situation where it is much easier for peripheral roles to be played without damaging the team effort. In time, members move from the periphery to the center and play a full part in achieving team objectives. The practice brings new blood to team building while ensuring continuity.

Ultimately, virtual teams embracing some of the elements of communities of practice can overcome, or at least minimize, many of the difficulties of operating in the distributed environment. Communications, relationships, cultural issues, and information and knowledge transfer can all be addressed by this mechanism, which is an additional weapon in the armory of teams.

Communications

A communications strategy is the final element in constructing a team-based virtual organization. It should include the following:

- Make one member of the team the knowledge manager.
- Initial team activity must be built around face-to-face communication to establish relationships. This must be repeated periodically.
- Categorize and prioritize the information to be communicated, and set appropriate conditions for dealing with each category.
- Communication must include comprehensive overviews of progress.

- Times and frequencies for regular communication should be established.
- Response times should be agreed and adhered to.
- Feedback and discussion must be built into the process, so this is another team responsibility to be allocated. A mediator will be required.
- Project timelines, whether in the form of Gantt charts, critical path analyses, or any other method appropriate to the task in hand, should be common property and available online. Scheduled log ins to view the data should be mandatory.
- Individual calendars or diaries should also be available.
- Set specific sessions for informal, non-work-related communications.
- Make certain that the informal sessions include celebrations—of birthdays, awards, good news of a business and personal nature.
- Failure to stick to the communication schedule should be investigated to avoid the possibility that some members will become sidelined.
- Each team member should accept the responsibility of informing all the others of their whereabouts and movements.
- Make use of multimedia—do not confine communication to text alone, but deploy Powerpoint and other software to add interest and clarity to what is being said.
- Tie the communication system into the broader information system. Integrate communication with the team-learning system so that all the knowledge or intelligence generated by the team activities is in the system.
- Extend the policies and the procedures to cover communications with other teams and the rest of the organization.

Managing Virtual Meetings

This may well be one of the most disconcerting aspects of distributed teams. Replacing the cut and thrust and the dynamics of face-to-face team meetings with a virtual environment without creating an anodyne and ineffective instrument of communication requires the implementation of a few more rules.

To begin with, in cyberspace the rules themselves change, behavior changes, and comfortable and well-known procedures go by the board. The following steps will help.

Retaining some of the useful conventions of corporeal meetings is an advantage. Send out a notification of the date of the meeting, and call for agenda items as if it were a traditional meeting. The documentation should be circulated in the usual way, but electronically. As far as the agenda is concerned, a procedure for tabling and circulating additional papers must be in place.

Set a date and time, but extend the period of the meeting over several days. This will make use of the flexibility of the virtual meeting and allow team members to fit the meeting in with their other activities. This should also allow for more time to reflect and consider and theoretically improve the standard of the contributions from individuals. The decision-making processes will then be improved through this ability to take more time over thinking things through.

Within the time slot, establish a time when all members will sign in, and a time at the end of the period when the meeting will close.

The actual conduct of the meeting itself requires some thought. There will still be a need for a traditional secretary to take notes, but these will be completed at regular intervals, with summaries of discussions circulated and action points noted and distributed.

The duties of the chairperson are also more complex, with a need to

- Ensure that all members of the team contribute. It is easier to hide in a virtual meeting, and without the advantages of the personal encounters, it may be more difficult to achieve maximum involvement.
- Maintain the timetable and ensure the decisions are actually taken. This appears on the face of it to be more difficult, but this might be another psychological effect of distributed meetings.
- Maintain the momentum of the meeting and the flow of the debate and discussion. For the same reasons given above, this is more difficult. In an important way, there is no flow and much less momentum in an electronic meeting.

One way of dealing with this is to use videoconferencing. Cheetham (2004) sets out the conditions and modus operandi for a system that, while operating within a more circumscribed and time-bound environment, can be used alongside conventional meetings as a counterweight to the virtual meetings that might dominate distributed team business.

The following case study examines a situation in which two organizations collaborated on the development of a virtual, distributed team to publish a professional journal. It demonstrates the key principles discussed in this chapter.

Case Study 2
MANAGING THE PUBLICATION OF VIRTUAL JOURNALS

The Situation

Threads was a professional journal published in both print and electronic formats and run by a consortium of the information services at two legal consultancy and training firms, Lawbooks and Gross. There was a small, distributed, full-time professional staff of three. It was funded by both organizations and was managed by two partners, one representing each company. The full-time staff comprised a managing editor, who as a freelance was located several hundred miles away from both organizations, and an editorial assistant and a freelance graphic designer, both of whom were based at Lawbooks and were largely responsible for the technical production of the print version of the journal. The technical aspects of the production of the electronic version of the journal were carried out by two members of the staff of Gross, who were also geographically separated from the other locations. The managing editor was responsible for editorial control and standards for both versions of the journal.

Relationships between the distributed team members were weak, and there were a number of contentious issues which contributed to the state of these relationships. In the first instance, the decision to create a consortium to jointly manage the print and web versions of the journal was not greeted with universal acclaim.

On the part of Lawbooks staff, there was a lingering resentment, even some three years after the creation of the partnership, that Gross had been foisted upon them, as they saw it, against their wishes. The latter, with a substantial reputation as a provider of legal training courses and consultancy services, considered themselves to be the natural senior partner in the alliance. Walter, the partner from Gross who represented the firm on the editorial board, was also an individual with considerable political power in professional circles.

This undercurrent was strengthened by the staff at Lawbooks, who rightly considered that their high-quality writing and page-design skills were undervalued by their fellow team members at Gross. They also considered, again with some justification, that their technical editorial skills were of a considerably higher order than those of their colleagues.

A further source of friction was the difference in underlying attitudes. At the time of the conception of the project, the idea of a parallel journal was new to the sector in which the publication was designed to operate, and the editorial team at Lawbooks had been inspirational and instrumental in bringing the proposal to fruition. They had also developed an innovative print version that had high production and content values that they felt were not matched by an error-strewn electronic version. There was a general feeling at Lawbooks that the electronic version of the journal did not make the best use of the medium, in terms of flexibility, innovation, currency, interactivity, and other matters. Giselle, the graphic designer at Lawbooks, had some experience and a successful track record as a Web designer. This expertise was available, and the designer wanted to share her skills, but proposals to collaborate across the boundaries of the two firms were ignored. Her input was therefore not utilized by the Web team at Gross.

There were also operational difficulties. The editorial assistant at Lawbooks worked full time on *Threads* and on other publications for Lawbooks, as did Giselle, the freelance graphic designer. The Gross staff involved took on the production of the electronic version as one of a number of other duties unrelated to the journal. Copy for the electronic version of the journal was made up of the print copy plus material added by the staff of Gross. This appeared in the electronic version only. Lawbooks staff were diligent in their adherence to the editorial schedule, but the electronic version rarely appeared on time because it was considered to be one of a number of responsibilities and was not given a high priority. When it did appear, the errors mentioned earlier were a source of friction, as was the general standard of the writing contributed by the staff at Gross.

Long-term objectives were also divergent. The more traditional Lawbooks members of the team were committed to the utility of a parallel publication, with the print version acting as an essential front end for the electronic version and supported a gradualist approach to the ultimate aim of producing a Web-only version of the publication. On the other hand, the technologically inspired Gross staff believed in an immediate move to an exclusively electronic journal. Equally significant, they were prepared to work behind the scenes to achieve this while maintaining an equable and committed front in public.

The manner in which this double-dealing came to light also caused some friction. Gross had experienced a difficult year as far as profits were concerned, and were seeking to make economies. They proposed to cut their contribution to *Threads* as one element in a program of retrenchment. Giselle, the graphic designer, during a videoconference with the senior Web editor at Gross, took some time to set out and explore the arguments for maintaining a print version of the journal. As the print version of the journal was self-financing from subscriptions and made a net contribution to the costs of the Web version, she felt that Gross's proposal would be a retrograde step. Within a few days, she received an e-mail from Walter, the senior partner at Gross, informing her that she had no right to continue to argue the case for a parallel publication when all it was likely to do was build up false hopes that things could continue as they were. This statement could only have been inspired by a report of the views she expressed during the videoconference and must have come from Simon, the senior editor at Gross.

Still on a personal level, there were other difficulties. The two staff based at Lawbooks quickly became aware that in fact all their conversations with their opposite numbers, especially comments or opinions they expressed about the future direction the publication should take, were being relayed immediately to the partner at Gross, Walter. They were then cross-examined on their views and given strong indications that strategic thinking was not their preserve.

There were other incidents that had a disruptive effect. On one occasion, a subscriber wrote a letter of complaint, commenting on a view expressed in an article in the print version and drawing attention to some errors in the Web version. The letter was emailed to the Web editor, who then corrected the errors in the Web version, deleted all references to them from the e-mail, and published the e-mail, now containing only the criticism of the print version, on the Website.

The Catalyst

Into this situation was pitched a new managing editor when the original freelance editor moved on. Surprised by the underlying feelings, he identified a number of issues that would have been damaging to a conventional team, but were even more potent sources of trouble in a virtual team.

Project Objectives

When the joint publication was established, the objective was clear:

- To create a parallel print and Web version of a professional journal that would
    - Demonstrate the best practice in the integration of a print and electronic publication in which each medium complemented the other
    - Introduce the readership to the advantages and strengths of a com-

plementary print and Web publication

- Gradually prepare for a transition from a parallel to an electronic-only publication

In reality, it very quickly became apparent that there were two agendas at work. The technologists at Gross clearly considered the print version to be little more than a generator of material for the electronic version. Their own barely articulated objective was to move as fast as possible to an electronic version and dispense with the print version. In this they were supported by the senior partner at Gross, who used the temporary cash flow problem as a lever.

There was also a lack of transparency in administrative matters. Although funding was provided by both firms on an equal basis, budgets were managed by the senior partner at Gross, and part of their contribution was paid in the form of time allocated to the publication by their two contributing team members. The Lawbooks partner was never able to ascertain what this contribution was actually worth and how much of the resource base was in fact being contributed by Gross. For their part, Lawbooks were open about the percentage of the costs they were contributing.

Varying Standards

For the new managing editor, there were more pressing matters. The weaknesses in the editorial procedures came to a head when he declined to publish a contribution he considered to be badly written and uninformative. Unknown to him, the article had also been submitted to the Web version editor, who published it unaltered. The resulting confrontation ended with the Web editor being forced to delete the offending article from the Web version. There was also a pointed exchange between the managing editor and the writer, made worse by the fact that unbeknown to the managing editor, the article had actually been commissioned by the Web editor.

Called to account for his actions, the managing editor had little choice but to defend his editorial responsibility to the two partners and made a spirited and reasoned argument in favor of the highest editorial standards, together with a principled statement of his views on editorial responsibility. In reply, the partner representing Gross reaffirmed his right, as the senior partner and the main stakeholder, at least in his eyes, to ultimate editorial control. The managing editor resigned immediately.

Within a short time, the partnership was dissolved and *Threads* became a Web journal.

Analysis

The problems revealed in this case study are a combination of the usual difficulties found in team organizations plus a number of others exacerbated by the distributed nature of the operation. The first one of these was that there was no attempt to create any kind of common ground between the two units. In no sense could they be described as a team. Separated by geography and attitude, there was no way in which an integrated whole could be created. The managing editor himself never met all the team members together, nor was there any consideration of the kinds of cross-organizational activities that might have created the sense of belonging to a single, unified team. Although there were skills in the Lawbooks team that complemented some of the technical skills of the Gross team, these common features were never allowed expression.

The main reason for this was that Gross retained ownership of the Web version in spite of the obvious links with the print version. This ownership extended to a refusal to allow the managing editor access to the website in order to ensure the effectiveness of the editorial processes.

Gross's sense of proprietary rights, reflected in other things like their attitude to the budget, stemmed from their view of their own position as the senior partner. What this suggests is a lack of equality in the relationship between the two teams.

The fact that one group was able to subvert the agreed objectives also suggests a lack of unity and a lack of transparency. The issue of trust emerges here as a key factor. Tied in with the mutual suspicion of each other's skills and competencies, there was very little chance that trust and confidence could develop. The lack of openness about the resource contributions of the two partners was another indicator.

Communication failures lay at the heart of the breakdown of the relationship. As indicated, the managing editor never met all members of the team together. The face-to-face contact was sporadic and was not supported by a proper communication strategy. For example, the organizations were well-equipped with videoconferencing facilities that were rarely used for the business of the journal. Virtual meetings were never attempted, and there was no protocol for using e-mail.

Here, the influence of the senior partner at Gross was again significant. His people skills were undeveloped. For example, thinking back over the time spent on this project, the managing editor realized that at no time, whether communicating face-to-face, on paper, or by electronic means, had the senior partner ever addressed him by name. The relationships that form the bedrock of communication never got off the ground, and the failure to use technology in an imaginative and organized way made matters worse.

Related to other broader issues, the lack of strategy and policy in the communications area meant that the communication that did take place was imprisoned within the confines of professional or technical matters. There was a failure to acknowledge the need to create a space for nonprofessional communication, and this hampered the development of rounded relationships that might have broken down the mistrust that existed.

The lack of a structured approach to communications was also characteristic of the information system. It simply did not exist, and there was in fact a complete lack of an information strategy. Because of this deficiency, there was no opportunity to use the complementary skills of the team members. Significantly, there was no chance of generating the creative abrasion that occurs when differing traditions, cultures, skills, and viewpoints are brought together. Professional exchanges were largely nonexistent, and there was no learning. Because neither side trusted the other in a general sense, nor had they real respect for each other's skills in some ways, there was no opportunity to develop self-management. This can only come when there is mutual confidence in the abilities of all the members of the team, and when all of the professional and personal standards are high enough to ensure the growth of proper self-discipline. The lack of trust prevented this from developing.

The vital early task of building relationships robust enough to survive in the distributed environment was ignored, apart from sporadic and formal meetings when specific issues had to be discussed. In particular, the essential building block of face-to-face communication was absent.

On a broader front, the general team-building process was seriously deficient. There was no effective selection process, and, with the exception of the managing editor, staff already in place were shoehorned into positions in the team. In one case at Gross, this process involved the insertion, for a short period, of a member of the team who was a problematic employee and was known not to possess the application nor the commitment to contribute effectively in the team environment. As time went by, it also became evident that no effort was being put into team maintenance. There was no learning process, and the essential skills of teamwork were not incubated.

It was also obvious with hindsight that a team culture failed to develop across the boundaries. While the Lawbooks team developed a team ethos with the small team around the managing editor, the same was not true of the Gross element of the team. Locked into a very powerful organizational culture driven by a strong personality with autocratic tendencies, the cross-boundary collaboration was not allowed to emerge.

Part of the problem was that the Gross faction saw no need to share. Exchanges between them and the other distributed members were formal, work based, structured, and largely to do with the mechanics of creating and transmitting files. There was no exchange of information about the creative activities of producing a parallel journal, and no exchange of expertise. While Lawbooks and the managing editor saw the cross-boundary collaboration as crucial, Gross did not.

At bottom, a unifying team culture did not develop. Concentrating solely on professional communications, a wider culture was stifled. There was no exchange of stories, no development of the small rituals that put a gloss on distributed teamwork, and no sharing of celebrations and other social situations. There was a failure to share either strategy or tactics.

Chapter 9

A Team Model

The Solution to Creating Virtual Teams

The list of problems to be overcome in developing virtual teams is an impressive one. The solutions lie in cultivating an approach that makes the best of what we already have while utilizing new technology and some more novel ideas about collaboration in organizations. This means first applying the key techniques of conventional team development. In other words, the task is to put in place a logical process of team building. It also means making the best use of the technology available. Both of these actions need to be linked with ways of increasing the degree of informal sharing between virtual teams. Finally, and most importantly, it means that we need to change the way we think of teams. This involves thinking in terms of new metaphors, and developing new models, for teams in information services.

The model of the individualized organization as proposed by Ghoshal and Bartlett (1998) is a useful one to consider. These two authors set out three tests that an organization fit for the 21st century should pass:

- Is it an appropriate environment for supporting individual creativity and encouraging individuals to show initiative?
- Can it support entrepreneurial activity?
- Can it renew itself?

If these tests are to be met, then certain other characteristics must be built into the organization. While it is true that bureaucracies might also exhibit delegation, and indeed innovation, these features are usually countered by rigorous control mechanisms, so the first and obvious condition is that the bureaucracy has to go. Control cannot be imposed from above. This shift of control must be accompanied by a downward shift of resources and responsibility in order to create true empowerment.

An open culture is a related prerequisite, and by this is meant a culture that encourages the questioning of accepted wisdom, double loop learning, and experimentation without fear of failure. The contention is that this will lead to an organic form of growth that will replace the carefully contrived structure of the divisional organization as found in most library services of any size.

Of perhaps greater significance, empowerment and decentralization also encourage a sense of ownership on the part of those involved, and thus ultimately leads to self-management. While engineering this shift, the organization needs to clarify what it is really about, for itself and for its users. Setting out the beliefs, the vision, the values, the strategy and the policies, and specifying attitudes and behavior is a crucial support for self-management. Without it, there is no adequate framework for behavior.

Implementation of the Model

Apart from the structural change referred to above, there are some less tangible steps to be taken. A team structure, being a cross-boundary device, clashes with the vertical divisions of a conventional organization. The team structure is also at odds with the flow of a conventional information system, so changing the direction of this is a primary task. The development of the horizontal information flow can be achieved in two ways:

- By nurturing cross-boundary roles. It is particularly important that managers undertake responsibility for issues that cut across the organization. This affords them the opportunity to communicate horizontally, both formally and informally. Tied in with an organizational learning function, cross-boundary roles should serve several purposes: They support learning and development, improve horizontal communication, build trust. It has often been pointed out that if managers or other staff wholeheartedly accept a coaching role, for example, there is an ancillary benefit in terms of the management of the organization's knowledge. The act of participating in coaching, or for that matter mentoring, leads to a consolidation of ideas on the part of the coach or mentor. While this is happening, knowledge that is tacit sometimes becomes formalized and recorded and so enters the organized base of knowledge

that is available to everyone.
- By making the organizational information system open to all. The technology to do this is well established, and what it takes is an acceptance by management that this openness will increase communication and develop the two-way trust between managers and managed that is essential to organizational health.

Modern organizations need to develop characteristics fit for the contemporary environment. They need to inculcate

- Learning
- Communication
- A sense of ownership
- Empowerment

There are a number of team models that offer some hope of this being achieved. It is worth reviewing here what virtual organizations will require of the team structures in order to fully match their organizational needs:

- A free flow of communication
- Less managerial control of communication
- Nurturing and championing of new ideas
- Every part of the organization, and every member of the team, must be totally visible to their fellow team members, and to other team members
- Sharing of expertise
- Universal access to the learning system and the fruits and rewards of learning
- The encouragement of shared leadership
- Adaptability, multiskilling, and the exploitation of all kinds of differences in skills, attitudes, and expertise
- A collaborative approach to strategy and policy formulation
- Multiple power centers
- Inspirational leadership engendering excitement, an appetite for taking responsibility, innovation, and trust

The major task is finding a model that will support all these ideas, difficult enough in traditional settings, and harder in situations where there is less face-to-face contact, noted earlier as one of the significant success factors in distributed learning. Environmental factors like the unpredictable technological impetus, the hybridity, the complexity, changes in user attitudes and information competencies, the threat of competition, cultural differences, and the need for collaboration will also present problems. As a result there is a special piquancy to the task of developing an organizational model on which 21st century libraries can be based.

The Antecedents

As suggested earlier, the history of distributed organizations goes back a long way, and there is little doubt that in many respects these ancient foundations contained at least some of the characteristics that we associate with modern libraries and the coming shape of information services. In some ways we are not in the least proposing a set of unique organizational circumstances. If we look at the history and characteristics of some of the organizations that developed into worldwide trading concerns, operating at least from the 17th century on, the managers of those great global organizations faced some of the problems increasingly faced by libraries today:

- The difficulty of managing without face -to -face contact.
- The problem of communication, limited as it was to the speed and stately motion of the slave-powered galley or square-rigged sailing vessel.
- The cultural differences between the center and the outlying countries. Even today textbooks still deal with issues like the dilemma of local versus expatriate recruitment which, in the light of earlier comments on creative abrasion and the importance of exploiting differences, is in fact not a dilemma at all.

There are also some already-mentioned references in the literature of management history to the character of the 15th century city-state of Venice acting even then as an international financier. What sort of systems did they employ in order to work across continents? Maybe they also had their technological answers. Whatever the situation was, there is no doubt that one aspect of the model for contemporary libraries must be technology.

The Technological Element

Allan (2004) deals with the problems of virtual teams in project management, referring to the increasing degree of teamwork across national boundaries and in different time zones. She also points out that some members involved in virtual teamwork could actually be working entirely on their own, heightening the need for support. Drawing on the work of Salmon (2000), she advocates a five-step model for virtual teamwork. This model combines communications technology with the need to communicate on social and personal levels. It sets out stages in which different considerations are highlighted, including access to the communications system, online socializing and information exchange, and the use of informal online communication as an important unifying activity.

The virtual team environment has also been supported by the development of appropriate software to underpin the needs examined briefly above. Amongst the better known are LotusNotes and Microsoft Exchange 2000. TeamIntelT 2004i (www.virtualglobal.com) is a recent addition to what is available. The use of the technology in this way is a significant part of the virtual team model. It provides a number of advantages in managing teams made up of permanent employees based in the same location, others on fixed term contracts, remote employees, and solo employees. Document sharing is facilitated, and coordination and collaboration can be improved. Developing a common purpose, while allowing team members the freedom to express themselves and manage their own business, is aided by the ability of the systems to monitor progress toward goals.

To these advantages can be added the benefits of the increasingly sophisticated e-mail management systems available. Many of these can be outsourced, relieving the organization and the teams of some administrative and technical burdens. This allows the teams to focus on the actual tasks and projects they are involved with. Muir (2004) describes the ultimate distributed experience—the office without walls, which has no fixed location and no real physical center.

Web-based systems using mobile devices also support out-of-office working. Some of the systems, such as Hexagon from HostEurope (www.hosteurope.de), also emphasize user friendliness and ease of setup and use for nontechnical staff. These can be key elements in the kind of teams that are likely to emerge. Taken together, the technology offers a number of features.

A Virtual Meeting Place

This is the space where much of the work is carried out. Team business can be logged, schedules can be monitored, and progress measured. It is also an area where things can be shared and where problem solving can take place. Issues can be discussed and collaboration can flourish across organizational and geographical boundaries. It is also important that social and personal issues receive some attention in this area.

An Aid to Teamwork

One of the dangers facing leaders of virtual teams is that of descending into the comfort zone of dispatching floods of e-mails in a desperate effort to maintain communication and ensure that everybody is kept in the loop. What this practice also ensures is overcommunication, an excess of information, disruption to schedules, and general frustration. The ability of the software to create visibility for all aspects of teamwork without an intrusive level of indiscriminate communication will add efficiency and reduce stress. It will also help create unity in a way that is impossible when communication is confined to an unimaginative use of e-mail or run-of-the-mill electronic document sharing. Web access can further enhance the process.

The other advantage of using team development software is that it will enable sophisticated information creation and sharing through document management and the broader availability of the full and formal record of team activity.

An Aid to Leaders

The pressing psychological difficulty for leaders of virtual teams is the problem of lack of physical reach. Most leaders, and probably all managers, would confess to some initial fears about loss of control in situations where there is little or no physical contact with team members, and there are certainly problems with motivation (see chapter 7). One of the major contributions of today's software is that it creates transparency, and the ability to see what is happening in distributed parts of the team is important for maintaining the direction and impetus of the work.

The Traditional Element

A vital early component of the model will be drawn from the conventional approach to teams. However effective the virtual communications referred to above, an element of face-to-face communication will always be a considerable advantage. This is particularly true during certain key stages of team growth:

- During the initial acclimatization stages when team behavior is developing. This is particularly true of the early period when teams are first formed.
- During those periods when the emergence of a coherent and unified approach faces a setback or when individual members regress.

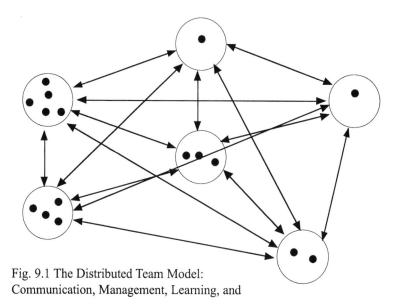

Fig. 9.1 The Distributed Team Model:
Communication, Management, Learning, and
Technological Patterns

- During a crisis, whether it is an issue with an individual as described above or to do with a failure to achieve an objective.
- At a moment of significant achievement. In the literature, much is made of the need to take advantage of virtual opportunities to celebrate personal and social situations. It is equally important to celebrate professional success—"looking for opportunities to praise" (Owen, 1996) —and this is one example where a real live meeting will pay dividends.

The Components

The proposed model is made up of a number of components:

- The learning system
- The technology
- Conventional communications
- A particular leadership style which is termed player management

In the model, teams and sole workers are linked into a network of the four components that are listed above.

The overall justification for using a team-based approach in the management of distributed organizations is based on the ability of teams to develop characteristics that will overcome the problem of separation. Properly managed, they can improve communication, they support learning, and they can be important motivational forces in distributed situations where some of the standard techniques of motivation might not be appropriate (but see also chapter 7). They can become self-renewing and will ensure continuity, and they ultimately improve management.

Outweighing all of these is the ability of the team to exploit differences. The virtues of teamwork center on unity, on improvements in communication, and on the development of leadership. Teams also maximize the utilization of skills and knowledge, and so improve decision making, flexibility, performance orientation, commitment and motivation, and trust. These attributes have been rightly emphasized in the literature, but it may well be that in the virtual and distributed environment, it is the capacity of the team to absorb and profit from differences, to channel varying perspectives and make capital out of the friction that will be the key to organizational health. Allan (2004) refers to examples of information services that already base more and more of their work on projects run by distributed teams working in different countries, in different time zones, and coming from different cultures. Some individuals may be working alone, while other parts of the team might enjoy the support of other members in the same physical location. The great strength of the team culture in these circumstances is its capacity to mold unity from this without stifling the creativity that comes from exploring differences, considering different approaches, and using cultural and professional differences in a positive way.

While team unity is rightly stressed, there is a downside to it in the possible emergence of groupthink. The model described here goes some way toward reducing this danger. Janis and others (1977) were amongst the first writers to identify this and described a pattern of behavior reflecting an unwillingness to consider any deviant views, an overwhelming belief in the rightness of group decisions, negative attitudes to outsiders, an enormous pressure to conform in every way, and a filtering of discordant information. This is the equal of the bureaucracy and effectively destroys the team. The model, by contrast, is based on the recognition and exploitation of differences. Other features described earlier, like communities of practice, can also weaken the power of groupthink.

There are a number of potential sources of conflict in cross-boundary working. These are to do with differing organizational cultures, individual differences and, in cross-national situations, differences in national cultures. Teams are settings in which the inevitable conflict over modus operandi, heightened by the distributed nature of the organization, can be managed positively as a source of organizational energy. Teams can accommodate most of the differences likely to be found in these situations and can use them productively.

Jazz Bands, Boats, Bombers, and Aerobatics

Do the Models Already Exist?

If we look hard enough, the answer is yes. This book has trumpeted the assertion that there is nothing new in managing distributed organizations, and the same can be said of teams. Group work, the crude forerunner of the team, has been common throughout the history of management. In a remarkably sophisticated form, the team itself is traceable through at least seventy years of organization management. Various management gurus have also used the metaphors of operas, orchestras, and jazz bands (see also chapter 3) in order to present a fresh view of how the organizations of the future should look—an important first step in considering the possibilities. The parallel with the jazz band, put forward by a number of authorities, is enticingly apposite. To develop it a little further, in jazz bands

- The musicians play a variety of different instruments
- Together they decide which compositions they will play and agree on the general shape of the orchestration
- They may well play their own distinctive variants of the tune
- The chances are that the piece will be performed in a different way each time it is played

The end result is a performance of some quality. Results are achieved apparently against all the odds and in spite of the differences in character, the degree of freedom all the players enjoy, and the opportunities for them all to interpret what they are doing in their own way. If these characteristics were transferred to library organizations, the result would be an organization that is

- Good at dealing with complexity, unpredictability, and diversity
- Capable of innovating
- Able to bring the best out of all the staff and use all abilities
- Distributed in terms of power
- Without a single center
- Supportive of players who are capable of both independent action and

close and effective collaboration
- Driven by an overall concept
- Imbued with some powerful motivational forces
- Fun to work in

The elements that are missing from the scenario above are those of the high technology environment. But even here there are precedents and examples that will help create an understanding of what sort of organizations we should be attempting to fashion.

Back to the Future

An organizational form that exhibits all the characteristics described in the chapters on teams existed as far back as the 1940s and perhaps reached its apotheosis during the period from 1943 to 1945. Some of the features established during this time have been honed and refined in contemporary practice in the same area of management. Owen (1996, 2001), analyzing the organization of the RAF aerobatics team, wrote of the "unique team-building techniques" of the Royal Air Force Red Arrows. These features were

- Selection based on both personality and skills
- Recruitment of new members as a team choice
- Self-criticism and the critical appraisal of others as an essential part of learning
- Good communication as a matter of priority
- The development of trust
- An emphasis on quality
- The ability to recognize their differences—"a team should be a collection of differences"
- Equal recognition of both personal and team needs and objectives
- No hierarchy
- Rewards based on recognition of the achievement of becoming a full member of the team
- A constant process of renewal as team membership changed on a regular basis

Of note, Owen indicated the absence of conflict, but maybe not friction, in this technology-rich environment. Team members considered that the quality of the communication, the openness and the constant self-appraisal and criticism of others actually removed the sources of conflict. In turn this made compromise unnecessary and replaced it with mutual agreement.

The basis for this kind of organization was laid down many years before the Red Arrows came into existence. If we turn the clock back to the 1940s, a similar approach to organizations emerges from an examination of World War II bomber crews. The seven-man crews of Lancaster Bombers demonstrated the same features identified by Owen 50 years later. They were

Rear Gunner   Navigator
                                     Engineer

          Mid-Upper Gunner

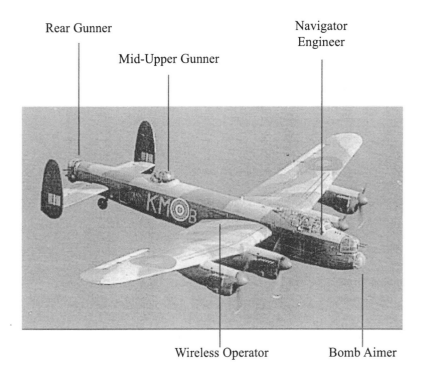

          Wireless Operator   Bomb Aimer

Fig. 9.2 A Team-Based Organization circa 1943

- Self-selection: Teams formed themselves, sometimes in the most unscientific but effective ways. Whenever the circumstances demanded, team members were often responsible for identifying and introducing replacements.
- Specialist yet multiskilled: Members were trained in their own roles and able to take over the jobs of other crewmen.
- Nonhierarchical: Like the Red Arrows, rank was irrelevant, with senior

officers not unusually flying under the command of flight sergeants.

- Practitioners of multiple leadership: Although the pilot was in overall control, different members of the crew took control at different times.
- Committed to learning: Crews underwent a massive amount of practice.
- Possessed of a very powerful culture that replaced the rule book to a certain extent: It is worth noting also that crewmen were all volunteers and could stop flying whenever they wished to without penalty other than an immediate transfer out of the squadron. One of the reasons they were able to continue to work in the most extreme situations was the strength of the culture.
- Unified: Through specialist teams organized across flights and the squadron, with strong boundary-spanning devices. Each position in the crew—pilot, engineer, navigator, radio operator, air bomber, and gunner, had its own team and team leader which integrated every specialization and also fulfilled a key learning function.

An advanced use of technology allowed all of these characteristics to be extended across boundaries. The model demonstrates the practical application of ideas about leadership, management styles, skills, learning, power, and responsibility. The communication and team management networks extend the structure across boundaries and underpin the virtual organization. Of equal importance, within the model are some ideas about how to deal with one of the least malleable issues in virtual organizations. This is the question of motivation, to which teams can make a significant contribution through the mutual support and cohesion they develop.

Mainstream literature on digital libraries continues to emphasize descriptions of specific programs, economic models, issues of implementation, communication in a technical sense, problems of scholarly publications, and access. It also covers topics like metadata and standards, and developmental issues are seen as centering on technical issues. Collier (2004) said,

> Those writing about the management of change always emphasize that the important factors are to do with people, not technology, or that the underlying principles of the profession, or user needs, or service quality are what really matter. Others may observe that despite the introduction of new technology, not much has changed. All these things may be true . . . the digital and the analogue will coexist for the foreseeable future. The author's criticism of this is that it is only a statement of the obvious . . . if one is trying to develop a theory or philosophy of the digital library, it does not help very much.

Postscript: Case Study 3
MANAGING THE 21st CENTURY
LIBRARY

The Background

During a reorganization, five medium-size colleges were amalgamated to create a single large metropolitan university. Five libraries, a reprographics and media service, a small Information Technology Unit and an Educational Television Service were combined in a Teaching and Learning Services Unit, and a Director of Teaching and Learning Services was appointed.

Vincent, the appointee, was formerly the Director of Learning Resources at a smaller college and before that had a background as a practicing professional librarian and a teacher of management. Although not inexperienced, this was his first major managerial post to date, and until that point he had adopted a conventional approach to management. This had been reflected in his approach to teaching management, and he had built a solid reputation that also provided some evidence of innovative skills and the ability to build an organization.

Two of the medium-size colleges that formed part of the new institution were prestigious in their fields.

Vincent's Approach

Vincent had one advantage. The new institution had called in an external specialist to advise them on the general shape of the new Teaching and Learning Services Unit prior to the appointment of the Director. This was a former colleague of Vincent's and the two were able to exchange ideas and views after the appointment had been made. Vincent was left in no doubt that he had accepted a major challenge, and his early observations of the situation confirmed this. For some time during his first term in office Vincent made no changes but continued to talk to colleagues within the service, teaching, and administrative staff, and students. The understanding that he faced a sustained period of organization development grew upon him. He also came to understand that his previous approach was not likely to produce the results he was looking for and had enjoyed in the past.

The Problems

The situation itself presented Vincent with some novel elements. He identified a number of potential difficulties.

Cultural Differences

The new service would be made up of eight previously autonomous units based in five totally independent institutions. Each head of service had enjoyed considerable freedom, but the status they were accorded within the former institutions varied considerably, and in some cases a resulting lack of resources and political influence had led to a defeatist and negative attitude. One organization was a typical hierarchical bureaucracy, rules-based and with a managerial culture. It was heavily influenced by contemporary university library practice, and the staff were not self-critical, but the other three libraries were in many ways typical primitive organizations. The personalities of the senior staff were naturally very different, and in Vincent's eyes one of the most notable features was the shortage of risk takers. There was little evidence of change or development over the years.

Professional Differences

There was a significant difference in professional standards between the five library services, and this reflected differing priorities. Some senior staff had sought strong formal links with teaching departments and as part of this accepted a prescribed input into teaching programs. This took time and, with comparatively small staff numbers, it meant that technical processes received less attention. This in turn led to backlogs in acquisitions and weak services in some areas.

Others had taken a more organic approach to faculty-library relationships and had been able to develop a strong and holistic relationship with library users, based on more than a formal approach.

Political Differences

The creation of the new institution had not met with universal acclaim, and one previously independent college had fought a strenuous but unavailing battle to stay outside it. The background of horse trading and attempts to protect interests that formed part of the merger negotiations inevitably carried over into the postmerger library reorganization, which was in any case one of the most tangible reminders of the merger. It soon became apparent that the idea of loyalty to a single institution and the integrated service Vincent was trying to create was a long way from the minds of some library staff at all levels. There was a clear tendency to look for leadership and advice to long-standing colleagues rather than to a new service director.

Resource Differences

This was both a help and a hindrance. Vincent clearly saw the problem of a lack of resources as a key factor related to the other issues described above. He also saw it as an opportunity to forge a new culture and new loyalties, provided that he could make progress towards an equitable and transparent resource allocation between the five campus libraries that would form the basic structure of the new service. He also realized that more resources would not automatically be provided by institutional management. This he saw as an advantage because of the opportunity it gave him to begin to develop an entrepreneurial culture.

The Approach

At first, Vincent felt that he had no template in his own experience that would give him any ideas about how to proceed in this situation. Taught management from a traditional point of view, he had worked in bureaucracies and managed one himself. But when he started to analyze his experience in his first serious managerial position, he realized that things were not quite as they appeared to be. Vincent had previously managed a small and resource-poor service. His way of dealing with this, making a virtue out of necessity, was to involve himself in the professional work of the library in areas where he had the expertise to contribute. Without fully understanding what he was doing and without really recognizing the term "player manager" except as something that applied to small, semiprofessional soccer teams, he had been making tentative steps in that direction. He began to educate himself in the concept and, relating these ideas to his analysis of the situation, he drew up a plan for organization development.

A Team Structure

Vincent decided to base the organization on teams. His first proposal was to break up the existing staff combinations and to create teams for each library based on service needs, staff attributes, and the potential to develop new skills. The previous heads of the five independent library services would become campus library team leaders. This served several purposes:

- It was the first step in forging a new culture encouraging loyalty to the new service rather than something based on old friendships and combinations that were likely to perpetuate the loyalty to former groupings.
- The teams would be related to service needs and not based on the existence of individuals in specific locations.
- Over time the structure would deliver the advantages of teams and would be a suitable construction for the risk-taking and entrepreneurial behavior Vincent wished to inculcate. In particular, it would strengthen the tradition of devolved responsibility that the campus librarians were in truth already used to as independent operators.

This team structure was to embrace previously separate areas of responsibility: Reprographics and Media Services and Information Technology were devolved to campus libraries as the old centralized operations were dismantled. A small central unit became responsible for acquisitions and procurement and administrative support. The result was the creation of multidisciplinary teams that provided the essential seedbed for creativity.

Communication

It was necessary to open communication channels between the five campus libraries. Dismantling the bureaucracy would change the communication structure that Vincent wished to replace with a more flexible system. Here he felt that the principles were more important than the methods. He wished to support self-management while ensuring the visibility of what went on in each of the campus libraries. To this end, he proposed a communications protocol that embodied the following principles:

- The library management system, together with the systems used in the media unit, was automated and the management statistics were made available to all service staff.
- All documentation except confidential personnel records were similarly a matter of public record. This included minutes of all meetings, planning documents, project reports and other information normally kept within the managerial purview. Documentation had to conform to an agreed format to ensure full disclosure.
- A protocol for using the university intranet was set up.

- Planning procedures, including budgeting and business plans, were made transparent and inputs solicited from all operational areas.
- The principles of devolved management were considered to be part of the communications process: Team leaders were expected to take decisions within the teams unless they had resource implications outside their devolved budgets or involved issues relevant to other teams. In these cases, proposed decisions were to be referred to the senior management team for comment and advice.
- The senior management team was reorganized to include other staff. Meetings were restricted to a maximum of once a month. Formal team meetings were similarly restricted, with the emphasis on formal, and the campus librarians established their own forum once again to meet formally no more than once a month and without the presence of the Director. In practice this was less frequent.
- Communication within teams was also systematized to ensure that all staff were aware of relevant issues, problems, and developments.

The informal communication system also received attention. Vincent very quickly identified key players in the informal communications system (see chapters 2 and 8). As part of his own role change, he developed a communication pattern to include these, and this was used to mutual and organizational advantage.

Role Change

As Vincent refined his ideas about player management, he realized that the basic principles, far from being applicable only to small-scale operations, were actually scalable and could be employed in much larger organizations, given careful preparation. He therefore turned his attention to the question of learning and development. Using the already established principle of participatory management, a comprehensive program of development was set up, concentrating in the first two years on team development, self-management, and the basic concept of player management. Over time this emphasis shifted, and a natural result was that within four years three unqualified members of the library staff whose roles had begun to change as a result of team working had completed professional qualifications. The corollary was the development of personnel policies that recognized development and facilitated the application of new skills and knowledge wherever relevant. Learning formed the bedrock of this. Vincent developed his own existing capacity for combining professional and managerial skills by involving himself in professional activities where his skills were relevant.

Conclusions: Cultural Change

Cultural change was the sum of Vincent's efforts. Staff were placed in teams that included other members who would otherwise have been separated because of the rigid organizational structure. New alliances were formed within the social network as well as within the team structures. Although the growth was not uniform, groups of staff began to develop problem-solving skills and propose creative and innovative solutions and developments. The time spent managing was reduced because of the broader involvement of staff outside the traditional management team and the growing ability of teams to manage their own affairs. There was also a recognition that large numbers of important decisions did not need to be taken within formal structures but were in reality capable of ad hoc resolution. Team responsibilities developed to include control of budgets, recruitment, and staff development and appraisal. Ideas about leadership were refined in practice and as part of a dynamic learning program. The amount of paperwork produced declined.

These things together created a new environment in which Vincent's risk-taking entrepreneurialism bore fruit in an unexpected way. The issue of scarce resources was identified and a number of revenue-earning schemes were put into operation.

Collaboration across organizations in the region also became a feature of library activity well before other more publicized schemes attracted attention. Informal links based on common concerns became stronger and stronger as time passed.

This was all achieved with less time spent on formal management, but the downside was indeed the question of time. The organizational change described in the past few pages took place over a period of some years. It also depended for its initial impetus on the happy coincidence of one or two like-minded people in the same place at the same time; there were other people who were made unhappy by the developments, never really accepted them, or did not settle in their new teams and eventually departed.

I would not claim that this particular book articulates a fully-fledged philosophy, but I would suggest that, the above case study apart, not much has changed on the ground, although perhaps not in the same way that Collier (2004) meant. Before we change things, we actually need a philosophy. It is perhaps contrary to end with the presentation of a metaphor for a new organization when that metaphor is drawn from something that existed over sixty years ago and is based on ideas that have been known to managers for at least the same length of time. But the strengths of the metaphor lie in the fact that it is to do with people and with underlying principles. As such, it will hopefully contribute to an understanding of how the key element of the people in organizations—both staff and users—fit into this technological landscape. The danger of an unbalanced approach to technology in information services, unaccompanied by policies and procedures for organization development that marry technological excellence and human skills, is that we will become involved in a crude form of business process engineering. This will amount to little more than an attempt to graft new and dynamic technology onto old organizations. In doing so, we will lose the human capital of tacit knowledge that is fostered by learning, communication, and the redefining of organizational shapes and roles, and we will fail to take advantage of the enormous benefits the technology can undoubtedly deliver.

It is fitting to conclude with two contrasting comments. The first is from a discussion document produced by a small university seeking to make savings of US$540,000 on their staff budget, and their views must therefore remain anonymous. They argued that

- Digital sources are replacing printed sources
- Online information retrieval is more effective than human searchers
- The skills and knowledge of academic staff could be used as a more effective way of strengthening the process of providing information
- Access and document delivery will permit staff reductions
- Technology will meet the needs of both local and distance users
- Information provision is being significantly deskilled through the development of online retrieval techniques

This particular set of assertions was used to effectively remove the majority of professional librarians working in face-to-face situations with users. The general justification put forward by management was that technology could replace the less efficient human beings who provided the information service for users. This could represent technological determinism. The opposing view was expressed by an academic at Johns Hopkins University:

> Our library has the most effective search engines yet invented: librarians . . . highly skilled at ferreting out the uniquely useful references. . . . Massive information overload is placing librarians in an ever more important role as human search engines. . . . Today's technology is spectacular — but it can't always trump a skilled human.
>
>   Have you hugged your librarian today?

                                                              (Brody, 2004)

Bibliography

Abrahamson, E. *Change without Pain: How Managers Can Overcome Initiative Overload, Organizational Chaos and Employee Burnout.* Boston, Harvard Business School Press, 2004.

Allan, B. *Project Management Tools and Techniques for Today's ILS Professional.* London, Facet, 2004.

Allee, V. *The Future of Knowledge: Increasing Prosperity through Value Networks.* New York, Elsevier Science, 2002.

Amabile, T., E. A. Schatzel, G. B. Moneta, and S. J. Kramer. "Leader Behaviors and the Work Environment for Creativity: Perceived Leader Support." *The Leadership Quarterly*, February 2004.

Andre, T. "Problem Solving and Education." InG. D. Phye and T. Andre (eds.) *Cognitive Classroom Learning: Understanding Thinking and Problem Solving.* Orlando, Harcourt Brace Jovanovich, 1986.

Auger, P., and J. Palmer. *The Rise of the Player Manager: How Professionals Manage as They Work.* London, Penguin, 2002.

Bass, B. M. *Bass and Stogdill's Handbook of Leadership.* 3rd ed. Glencoe, Free Press, 1990.

Bateson, G. *Steps to an Ecology of Mind.* London, Ballantine, 1972.

Belbin, R. M. *The Coming Shape of Organisation.* Oxford, Butterworth Heinemann, 1998.

Belbin, R. M. *Management Teams.* New York, John Wiley & Sons, 1981.

Belbin, R.. M. T*eam Roles at Work.* Oxford, Butterworth-Heinemann, 1993.

Bennis, W. "Good Managers and Good Leaders." *Across the Board* 21, part 10, October 1984.

Brewerton, A. "Have a Break, Have a Kitkat." *Multimedia Information and Technology* 29, no. 1, February 2002.

Brickley, J. A., C. W. Smith, J. Willet, and J. L. Zimmerman. *Designing*

Organizations to Create Value: From Strategy to Structure. New York, McGraw-Hill, 2003.

Brock, D., M. Powell, and C. R. Hinings. *Restructuring the Professional Organization*. London, Routledge, 1999.

Brodsky, N. [Interview in] *Inc* 22, issue 10, 2000.

Brody, W. R. "Thinking Out Loud." *The JHU Gazette: The Newspaper of the Johns Hopkins University* 34, no. 14, December 6, 2004.

Brophy, P., S. Fisher., and Z. Clarke. (eds.) *Libraries without Walls: The Delivery of Library Services to Distant Users*. London, Facet, 2002.

Bryson, J. *Effective Library and Information Centre Management*. 2nd ed. Aldershot, Gower, 1999.

Bucknall, T. "Techno Teamwork: Involving All Library Staff in Library Automation." *North Carolina Libraries* 54, no. 4, 1996.

Burnes, B. *Managing Change: A Strategic Approach to Organisational Development and Renewal*. 4th ed. London, FT/Prentice Hall, 2004.

Burns, T., and G. M. Stalker. *The Management of Innovation*. London, Tavistock Press, 1961.

Carr, D. K., K. J. Hard and W. J. Trahant. *Managing the Change Process*. New York, McGraw Hill, 1996.

Cheetham, K. "Practical Tips on Setting up a Videoconferencing Studio." *Multimedia Information and Technology* 30, no. 1, May 2004.

Child, J. (ed.) *Man and Organization: The Search for Explanation and Social Relevance*. London, Allen and Unwin, 1973.

Chowdhury, G. G., and S. Chowdhury. *Introduction to Digital Libraries*. London, Facet, 2003.

Clegg, S. (ed.) *Working Papers on Library Staffing Structures*. London, Society of College National and University Libraries, 2003.

Clutterbuck, D., and S. Kernaghan. *The Power of Empowerment*. London, Kogan Page, 1994.

Collier, M. "After the Digital Library Decade: Where Are the Next Frontiers for Library Innovation?" In Andrews, J. and D. Laws. (eds.) *Digital Libraries: Policy, Planning and Practice*. Aldershot, Ashgate, 2004.

Cox, R. H. *Sports Psychology: Concepts and Applications*. New York, McGraw-Hill, 2002.

Cross, R. "Who Talks to Whom about What." *Trends and Ideas* 1, no. 1, Fall 2003.

Cross, R., and A. Parker. *The Hidden Power of Social Networks*. Boston, Harvard Business School Press, 2004.

Curtis, D. (ed.) *Attracting, Educating, and Serving Remote Users through the Web*. London, Facet, 2002.

Cutting, A. *The Changing Nature of Work in Library and Information Services.* M.Sc. thesis, Department of Information Studies, University of Wales Aberystwyth, 2002.

Dale, A. "Transforming the Future of Library and Information Science Units." *The Nordic Journal of Documentation* 58, no. 1, 2003.

De Geus, A. *The Living Company.* Boston, Harvard Business School, 2002.

Dearnley, J., and J. Feather. *The Wired World: An Introduction to the Theory and Practice of the Information Society.* London, Library Association Publishing, 2001.

Deci, E. L., and R. M. Ryan. "A Motivational Approach to Self: Integration in Personality." In R. A. Dienstbier (ed). *Perspectives on Motivation. Nebraska Symposium on Motivation.* Lincoln, University of Nebraska Press, 1991.

Delphi. Report on Remote Library Services. 2002. Available: http://www.tls.se/kurser_konferenser/iok/2002/delphi_results.lasso

Deming, W. E. *Out of the Crisis.* Cambridge, Cambridge University Press, 1986.

Donkin, R., *Blood, Sweat and Tears.* New York, Texere, 2001.

Drucker, P. F. *Managing in the Next Century.* New York, St. Martin's Press. 2002.

Drucker, P. F. "What Makes an Effective Executive." *Harvard Business Review* 82, no. 6, June 2004.

Fayol, H. *General and Industrial Management.* Translated from the French edition (Dunod) by Constance Storrs, with a foreword by L. Urwick. London, Pitman, 1971.

Follett, M. P. *The New State: Group Organization: the Solution of Popular Government.* New York, Longmans, 1918.

Follett Report: *Joint Funding Councils' Libraries Review Group Report.* (Chairman Professor Sir Brian Follett). London, Higher Education Funding Council for England, 1993.

Geryts, E. D. "Organisational Transformation." *IATUL Proceedings (new series)* 4, 1995.

Ghoshal, S., and C. Bartlett. *The Individualized Corporation: A Fundamentally New Approach to Management.* London, Heinemann, 1998.

Glass, N. *Management Masterclass: A Practical Guide to the New Realities of Business.* London, Nicholas Brealey, 1996.

Gorman, M. "Bibliographic Control or Chaos: An Agenda for National Bibliographic Services in the 21st Century." *67th IFLA Conference and General Conference.* August 16-25, 2001.

——. "On Doing Away with Technical Services Departments." *American Libraries* 10, July-August 1979.

Gouillart, F. J., and J. N. Kelly. *Competing for the Future*. New York, McGraw Hill, 1995.

Gratton, K. *The Democratic Enterprise*. London, Financial Times/ Prentice Hall, 2004.

Griffiths, A. *Digital Television Strategies: Business Challenges and Opportunities*. Basingstoke, Palgrave Macmillan, 2003.

Gryskiewicz, S., and S. Taylor. "A Path to Success: The Practical Truth of Creativity." *Training Journal*, November 2003.

Hammer, M. "Deep Change: How Operational Innovation Can Transform Your Company." *Harvard Business Review* 82, no. 4, April 2004.

Handy, C. *The Age of Unreason*. London, Arrow Books, 1995.

Harrison, C. T. "Writing a Professional Development Report." In Wood, K. (ed.) *A Chartership Reader*. London, Career Development Group, Library Association, 2000.

Heckhausen, H. (tr P. K. Lepmann) *Motivation and Action*. Berlin, Springer Verlag, 1991.

Hersey, P., K. H. Blanchard and W. E. Natemeyer. "Situational Leadership, Perception and the Impact of Power." *Group and Organizational Studies* 4, part 4, December 1979.

Hersey, P., and J. Stinson. *Perspectives in Leader Effectiveness*. Ohio, Ohio University Press, 1980.

Herzberg, F. *The Motivation to Work*. London, Granada, 1959.

Hirshberg, J. *The Creative Priority*. Harmondsworth, Penguin, 1998.

Huczynzki, A. A., and D. Buchanan. *Organizational Behaviour: An Introductory Text*. 4th ed. New York, Pearson Education, 2001.

Janes, J. *Introduction to Reference Work in the Digital Age*. New York, Neal-Schuman, 2003.

Janis, I. L., and L. Mann. *Decision Making: A Psychological Analysis of Conflict, Choice, and Commitment*. New York, Free Press, 1977.

Katzenbach, J. *Real Change Leaders*. London, Nicholas Brearley, 1996.

Kimble, C., F. Li and A. Barlow. *Effective Virtual Teams Through Communities of Practice*. Research Paper 2000/9. Glasgow, University of Strathclyde Business School, 2000.

La Barre, P. "The Agenda—Grassroots Leadership." In Taylor, R. L., and W. E. Rosenbach. *Military Leadership: In Pursuit of Excellence*. Boulder, Westview, 2000.

Lancaster, F. W. *Indexing and Abstracting in Theory and Practice*. 3rd ed. London: Facet, 2003.

Lankes, R.D., C.R. McClure, M. Gross, and J. Pomerantz, (eds.) *Implementing Digital Reference Services: Setting Standards and Making It Real*. London, Facet, 2003.

Lave, J., and E. Wenger. *Situated Learning: Legitimate Peripheral Participation*. Cambridge, Cambridge University Press, 1991.

Lawrence, P. R., and J. W. Lorsch. *Organization and Environment*. Boston, Harvard Business School, 1967.

Lewin, K. *Field Theory in Social Sciences*. London, Tavistock, 1952.

Library and Information Commission. *New Library: The People's Network*. London, DCMS. 1997.

Liden, R. C., and G. Graen. "Generalization of the Vertical Dyad Linkage Model of Leadership." *Academy of Management Journal* part 23, 1980.

Lipman-Blumen, J. *The Connective Edge: Leading in an Independent World*. New York, Jossey-Bass, 1996.

Lynch, B. (ed.) *Management Strategies for Libraries: A Basic Reader*. New York, Neal-Schuman Publishers Inc., 1985.

Marcum, D. "Requirements for the Future Digital Library." *The Journal of Academic Librarianship* 29, no. 5, September 2003.

Marquandt, M. J. and G. Kearsley. *Technology-Based Learning: Maximizing Human Performance and Corporate Success*. New York, CRE Press, 1999.

Martell, C. *The Client-Centered Academic Library*. Westport Ct., Greenwood Press, 1983.

Maslow, A. H. "A Theory of Human Motivation." *Psychology Review* 50 (1943).

McInerney, D. M., and V. McInerney. *Educational Psychology: Constructing Learning*. 2nd ed. Sydney, Prentice Hall, 1998.

Mintzberg, H. *The Structure of Organizations*. New York, Prentice Hall, 1979.

Morgan, G. *Images of Organization*. New ed. London, Sage, 1997.

Muir, G. "Offices Without Walls." *Multimedia Information and Technology* 30, no. 4, November 2004.

Nutt, P. C: *Why Decisions Fail: Avoiding the Blunders and Traps That Lead to Debacles*. New York, Berrett-Koehler, 2002.

Owen, H. *Creating Top Flight Teams*. London, Kogan Page, 1996.

———. "Leading the Way in the Way of Leadership." *Western Mail* (27th January 2001).

Palmer, J. "Heaven and Hell: Surviving Self-Organizing Teams." *Journal of High Performance Teams* 3, no. 4, August 1998.

Pantry, S., and P. Griffiths. *Your Essential Guide to Career Success*. London, Facet Publishing, 2003.

Pearn, M., and C. Mulrooney. *Tools for a Learning Organisation*. London, Institute of Personnel and Development, 1995.

Pearn, M., C. Roderick and C. Mulrooney. *Learning Organizations in Practice*. New York, McGraw-Hill, 1995.

Peters, T. J., and R. H. Waterman. *In Search of Excellence: Lessons From America's Best Run Companies*. New York, Harper and Row, 1982.

Potter, E. H. III., W. E. Rosenbach, and T. S. Pitttman. "Followers for the Times: Engaging Employees in a Winning Partnership." In Rosenbach, W. E., and R. L. Taylor. *Contemporary Issues in Leadership*. Boulder, Westview, 2001.

Pugh, L. "The Calm of My Life Ended There." *Multimedia Information and Technology* 29, no. 2, May 2003.

———. *Change Management in Information Services*. Aldershot, Gower, 2000.

———. *Convergence in Academic Support Services*. London, British Library Research and Innovation Report, British Library, 1997.

———. "Designing Library Organisations for the E-future." *The Nordic Journal of Documentation* 58, no. 1, 2003a.

———. *Leadership and Learning: Helping Libraries and Librarians Reach Their Potential*. Lanham, MD, Scarecrow Press, 2001.

———. *The Management of Innovation in Public Sector Higher Education Learning Resources Provision, 1972 to Date*. Leeds, Leeds Metropolitan University, M.Phil. thesis, 1990.

———. *Organizational Structures in Converged Information Services*. Unpublished small-scale research project, February 2002.

———. *The Organisational Design and Development of Hybrid Libraries: Structures, Leadership, Management Styles and Philosophy, Professional and Personal Development*. London, Library and Information Research Group, 2004.

Putnam, R. D. *Bowling Alone: The Collapse and Revival of American Community*. New York, Simon and Schuster, 2000.

Raitt, D. (ed.) *Libraries for the New Millenium*. London, Library Association Publishing, 1997.

Raymond, E. S. "The Cathedral and the Bazaar." *Firstmonday*. www.first-monday.dk/issues/issue3 3/raymond/ 1998.

Renshon, S. A. "Governing a Divided America in the New Millenium." In Valenty, O. L., and O. Feldman. *Political Leadership for the New Century: Personality and Behavior Among American Leaders*. Westport CT, Praeger, 2000.

Roberts, M. J. "The Winds of Change: A Conversation with Professor

Mary Tripsas." *New Business*, Spring 2004.

Rollins, H. (ed.) *Letters of John Keats*. 2v. Cambridge, CUP, 1958.

Rose, S. *The 21st Century Brain: Explaining, Mending and Manipulating the Mind*. London, Jonathan Cape, 2005.

Salmon, G. *E-moderating*. London, Kogan Page, 2000.

Sapp, G. "The Context for Access Services." *Journal of Access Services* 1, no. 1, 2002.

Sashkin, M., and W. E. Rosenbach. "A New Vision of Leadership." In Taylor, R. L., and W. E. Rosenbach, (eds.) *Military Leadership: In Pursuit of Excellence*. Boulder, Westview, 2000.

Schmidt, W. D., and D. A. Rieck. *Managing Media Services: Theory and Practice*. 2nd ed. Englewood, Libraries Unlimited, 2000.

Senge, P. M. *The Fifth Discipline: The Art & Practice of the Learning Organization*. London, Century Business, 1993.

Simpson, P., R. French, and C. E. Harvey. "Leadership and Negative Capability." *Human Relations* 55, no. 10, October 2002.

Stueart, R. D., and B. Moran. *Library and Information Center Management*. 6th ed. Greenwood Village, Libraries Unlimited, 2002.

Stogdill, R. M. *Handbook of Leadaership*. Glencoe, Free Press, 1974.

Su, S. S. "Web-based Reference Services: the User-intermediary Interaction Perspective." In G. E. Gorman (ed.) *The Digital Factor in Library and Information Services* (International Yearbook of Library and Information Management 2002/2003). London, Facet, 2002.

Terris, O. "Chaos in Compromise." *Multimedia Information and Technology* 29, no. 3, May 2003.

Town, J. S. "Information Literacy and the Information Society. " In Hornby, S., and Z. Clarke (eds.) *Challenge and Change in the Information Society*. London, Facet, 2003.

Tuckman, B. W. Developmental sequence in small groups. *Psychological Bulletin*, no 63, 384-389, 1965.

Valenty, L. O., and O. Feldman. *Political Leadership for the New Century: Personality and Behavior Among American Leaders*. Westport, Praeger, 2000.

Verspagen, B., and C. Werker. T*he Invisible College of the Economics of Innovation and Technical Change*. Eindhoven, University of Eindhoven, 2003.

Walters, R., and C. Macrae. "Knowledge Management: What Lies Ahead?" *Training Journal* August 2003.

Watson, L. "Coffee, Computers and Cooperative Learning." *Multimedia Information and Technology* 29, no. 1, February 2003.

Weber, M. *Theory of Social and Economic Organization.* New York, Free
    Press, 1947.

Wiberg, L. E. "Should You Change Your Leadership Style?" *Management
    Solutions* January 1988.

Wilder, S. "The Changing Profile of Research Library Professional Staff".
    *ARL: A Bimonthly Report on Research Library Issues and Actions from
    ARL, CNI, and SPARC* no. 208/209, Feb./Apr. 2000.

Zafeiriou, G. "Managing Online Conflict and Reaching Consensus in Text-
    based Computer Conferencing: The Student's Perspective." *Education
    for Information* 21, 2003.

Index

abrasion, creative. *See* creative abrasion

access services, 15

amalgamation, cultural differences, 190; information services, 189-95; political differences, 190; professional differences, 190; team structure, 191-92

assessment, learning process, 87-88

attitudes, managerial, 52-53, 67-68, 85-86, 117-32

autocracy, and player managers, 128

behavior, managerial. *See* attitudes, managerial

behaviorist approach, leadership, 100

bureaucracy, and distributed organizations, 38-41, 81-83, 150-58, 190

bureaucracy, and innovation, 48, 106-7

bureaucracy, and structures, 48-49, 81-83, 130-31, 134-35, 177-78, 190

bureaucratic management, 25-27, 50, 54, 59-61, 65-66, 81-83, 117-18, 130-31, 134-35, 147-49, 177-78, 184, 190; and communication, 63-67, 81-83

cataloguing skills. *See* skills, cataloguing

change instruments, 53

change, in work conditions, 126-27

change management, 84-86; misnomer, 96-98

charisma, leadership, 102-4, 106, 111-12

circle structure, 66

coercive power, and leadership, 101-2

cognitive power, leadership, 113

collaboration, and communication, 71-72, 170-76; and cross-boundary devices, 71; and equality, 71; and leadership, 107, 110-11; and mutuality, 71; digital, 87, 150; interlibrary, 69-73, 81-83, 170-76; staff, 52, 165; virtual library, 83-84; with the enemy, 83-84

collaborative projects, 69-73, 166

collection management, 12

communication, 63, 65-66, 79, 112, 132, 136-37, 170-76; and leadership, 102-4; and networks, 40-41, 43-45, 71-72, 79, 95-96, 188; and teams, 151, 154-56, 167-68, 170-

76, 188, 190-93; formal, 64, 192-93; frameworks, 54, 132; informal, 63-64, 193; managerial skills, 91-92; social aspects, 79

communities of practice, 166-67, 184

competition, 19-20; and motivation, 134-35; organizational health, 83

complex structures, 18-19; technologies, 11

complexity, 11-12

computer conferencing, 82

consensus, in organizations, 26-27

conservatism, 24, 28

contemporary organizations, characteristics, 3-24, 26, 28-29, 31-32, 33-34, 42, 49-52, 85-86, 179; and creativity, 88-89; and leadership, 107-12; and teams, 145-95

contingency approach, and leadership, 100-1

contingency theory, 36-37

continuing development, and virtual teams, 163-64

creative abrasion, 43,56-57, 68

creative friction, 68

creativity in organizations, 42-45, 62, 69-73, 83, 86, 88-89

cross boundary devices, and teams, 178-80, 184-85; in collaboration, 71

cultural change, 57, 194-95

cultural engineering, and leadership, 113-14

culture, open, 178

culture, organizational. See organizational culture

decision making, 51-53, 57, 85, 90, 104-6; imaginative-analytical, 104-5; structural, 105; traditional, 105; distributed, 49

deskilling. See skills, deskilling

detail, attention to by player managers, 129

determinism, technological. See technological determinism

dialog, staff and user, 94

differences, and organizational development, 9

digital technology, and libraries, 4-6, 11, 37-38, 82, 95-98, 188

digitization. See digital technology

distributed decision-making centers, 49

distributed organizations, 69-73, 81-83, 149. See also bureaucracies and distributed organizations

distributed teams, and communities of practice, 166-67; information system, 159-60; learning, 166-67; model, 183-85; problems, 153-60, 166; psychological problems, 158-59, 166

double loop learning, 32

economy, mixed, in information services. See mixed economy, information services

electronic library, 4-10, 12-22, 28-29, 30-32, 43-45, 60, 80-81, 95-98, 145-46, 168-76; communication, 91-92, 155-56, 158-59, 168-69; creativity, 42-45, 58; design, 52-53; teams, virtual, 160-69, 181-82

electronic mail, 95, 137, 155-56, 158-59, 181-82

e-mail. See electronic mail

empowerment, 99-116

equality, in collaboration, 71

expectancy theory, 137-39

expectations, and change, 28-29

experience, learning from. See learning from experience

experimentation, and player managers, 125
expert power, and leadership, 101

flat structures, motivation, 133-34, 140-42, 161
flexibility, in management, 117-18; in organizational structures, 68
friction, creative. *See* creative friction
functional organizations, 27

hub and spoke structures, 65-66
human relations school, 26-31
hybrid library, characteristics, 8, 10, 34-38, 49, 55, 62-63, 88-89, 94-96, 98, 107, 109-11, 115, 120-21, 133-42, 150-51; motivation in, 133-42; teams in, 150-51, 157-95
hybridity. *See* hybrid library
hygiene factors, motivation, 137, 141-42

incentives, motivation, 133-34
individual learning, 86-88, 93-94, 97-98, 148
influential power, 102-4
information flow, 90-92; in teams, 67
information services, amalgamation, 189-95; contemporary, leadership, 107-12; structure, 38-41, 61, 66-68, 117-32; subsystems, 29-30, 64; technology, 79-90. *See also* hybrid library, characteristics
information society, changes, 7-8, 10-11
information systems, distributed teams, 159-60; management, 84-86; information technology in, 84-86, 95-98
integrated collections, 18
integrated networks, 82, 84-85
Internet, and libraries, 4, 12, 28, 95-96
intrinsic motivation, 140-42

invisible college, 166-67

jazz bands, team model, 185-86
job enrichment, 43-45

knowledge architecture, 86-88
knowledge dissemination, 67
knowledge management, 32-35, 60, 159-60
knowledge revolution, 5-6

Lancaster Bomber, team model, 187-88
leaders, as cultural engineers, 113-14; modern, characteristics, 113; team, 130, 162, 182
leadership, 93, 99-116, 123, 136; and empowerment, 99-116; and player managers, 130; and power, 101-4, 113; behaviorist approach, 100; charisma, 102-4, 106, 111-12; contingency approach, 100-1; decision making, 104-6; in bureaucracies, 50; in partnerships, 108-11; in teams, 111-12; organizational characteristics, 107-12; path goal theory, 104; reactionary, 106; situational approach, 100-1; theory, 99-101; trait approach, 99-100; transactional, 106-7; transformational, 106-7; visionary, 112-13
learning, and individuals, 30-31, 86-88; facilitators, 53-54, 87-88; from experience, 90-93; managed, 87-88, 97-98, 193; organizational, 89, 97-98, 132, 193
Learning Café project, Glasgow Caledonian University, 8
learning organizations, and libraries, 31-32, 53-54, 87-88; objectives, 32
learning process, and teams, 87-88, 146; assessment, 87-88; conceptual

framework, 86-88; new approach, 90-92
learning skills, 77-98
learning system, organizational, 88, 132
legitimate power, 101-4

managed learning. *See* learning, managed
management information systems, 84-86
management teams, 152-53
managerial attitudes, 52-53, 67-68
matrix structures, 61-62
meetings, virtual, 169-70; videoconferencing, 169-70
middle management, 92-93
military management, influence of, 25
mixed economy, libraries, 8-10
motivation, 133-42; and competition, 134-35; and flat structures, 133-34, 140-42, 161; and organizational characteristics, 133-37; and power, 134-36; and self-worth, 139-40; and status, 134-35; expectancy theory, 137-39; higher order needs, 134-35; hygiene factors, 137, 141-42; in teams, 161-62, 188; incentives, 133-34; individual, 139-40; intrinsic, 140-42; modeling, 136-37; rewards, 135-36
multiskilling, 80-81
mutuality, in collaboration, 71

negative capability, xii-xiii
network analysis, 40-41, 49-50, 81-83
networks, and technology, 78; characteristics, 66-68, 83-84; integrated, 82, 84-85; interlibrary, 70-73, 150; living, 59-60, 65-68; social, 39-41, 49, 50-52, 54-55, 57, 60, 66-67, 79, 81-83, 166-67, 194-95

open systems theory, 29-30
organic systems, 36, 58-60, 67
organizations, as brains, 55, 59, 82; as machines, 24-26; living, 36, 58-60, 67
organization development, 30-31, 130, 138-39; and distributed teams, 153-60; and player managers, 130; characteristics, 31, 54, 138-39, 164; methodologies, 138-39
organizational architecture, xii, 50, 81-83
organizational creativity, 42-45, 46-47, 62, 69-73, 83, 86, 88-89, 131
organizational culture, 113-14; 117-32, 134-35, 150-58
organizational health, ix-xiii, 29-30, 49, 132, 137, 141-42; and competition, 83
organizational learning, 89, 90-92, 97-98; systems, 88
organizational redundancy, 43-45, 55-59, 83
organizational structures, xiii, 4-5, 9, 11, 38-41, 47-73; and leadership, 99-116; and multiskilling, 80-81; and player managers, 117-132; and power, 101-4; as indicators, 52-54; complexity, 10-11; flexibility, 68; functionally based, 27, 59-60; importance of, 52-54; options, 61-63; problems with, 48-50; process-based, 61; traditional, 11, 24-25, 27, 48-49. *See also* matrix structures
organizations, and creativity, 42-45; virtual, 149-50; and ownership, 43-45, 57

partnerships, 108-11
path goal theory, 104
performance, and player managers, 127

peripheral participation, teams, 167

personalization, library services, 12-13

player managers, 117-32, 149; and autocracy, 128; and experimentation, 125; and learning, 132; and objectivity, 128; and performance, 127; and sharing, 124-25; and structural change, 132, 193; and team building, 132, 152-53, 161, 165-66, 193; characteristics of, 120-21; dangers of, 128-30; development of, 130-32; roles and functions, 124-28; values, 126-28

power, and leadership, 113; and motivation, 134-36

process-based teams, 153

process-based structures, 61

professional skills. *See* skills, professional

project teams, 56-57, 83, 153, 166, 170-76

reactionary leadership. *See* leadership, reactionary

Red Arrows, team model, 186-88

redundancy, organizational. *See* organizational redundancy

resource sharing. *See* collaboration, interlibrary

rewards, motivation, 135-37

self-management, in virtual teams, 165-66

self-worth, motivation, 139-40

single loop learning, 32

situational leadership, 100-1

skills, and deskilling, 79-80; and multi-skilling, 80-81; and specialization, 13-19, 30-31, 33, 35, 41, 49, 56, 58, 61, 73-98, 135-37, 153; and technology, 78-90; cataloging, 80; changing, x-xi, 30-31, 33, 35, 41, 49, 56, 73-98; communication, 91-92; learning, 77-98; management, 77-98; new, 13-19, 30-31, 33, 35, 41, 49, 56, 58, 61, 73-98, 135-137, 153

skills, professional, 93

skills, reinvigorating, 90-92

skills, traditional, 79-80, 90-92

social networks. *See* networks, social

specialization, and matrix structures, 61-62; and new skills, 13-19, 30-31, 33, 35, 41, 49, 56, 58, 80-81, 93-98, 107

staff, and users, 93-98; motivation, 138-39; structures, 15-17, 18-19, 93-98

structured decision making. *See* decision making, structured

structures. *See* organizational structures

structures, system-based. *See* system based structures

systems theory, 29-31

systems-based structures, 63

teams, 53, 58, 62-64, 66-68, 83, 93, 105, 107-11, 119-20, 125-26, 128-29, 145-95; amalgamation, 191-92; and cultural change, 193-94; and player managers, 117-32, 152-53, 161, 165-66; communication, 157, 154-56, 167-68, 170-76, 192-93; communities of practice, 160-67; distributed, 151-60, 166-67, 183-85; hybrid library, 150-51, 157-60; incentives, 133-36; information flow, 67; learning process, 87-88; legitimate peripheral participation, 167; model, 177-95; leaders, 182; management, 152-53; problems, 147-149, 160; project, 56-57, 83, 153, 167; role change, 193; tradi-

tional, 147-49, 160-69; virtual, 156-
169, 170-76, 177-95
technological determinism, 7-8
technologies, complex. *See* complex
technologies
technology, and virtual teams, 160-69,
180-82; information, 84-86. *See
also* digital technology
thinking, unconventional. *See* thinking
outside the box
thinking outside the box, 37-38, 43, 85
traditional library organizations, 11, 24-
25, 27, 39, 41-45, 63-68, 79, 97,
117, 131, 134-35; and player managers, 120-21; leadership in, 106-
11, 131; and teams, 147-49, 150-51,
160-69, 180
trait approach, leadership, 99-100
transactional leadership, 106-7
transformational leadership, 106-7

uncertainty in library organizations, xii-xiii
unconventional thinking. *See* thinking
outside the box

unpredictability in libraries, 20-21
user-staff relationships, 93-98; dialog,
94; demands, 94

values, player manager, 127-28
videoconferencing, virtual meetings,
169-70
virtual journals, case study, 170-76
virtual meetings, management of, 168-
69; videoconferencing, 169-70
virtual organizations, 149-50, 168-69
virtual teams, 156-69; continuing development, 163-64; control and management, 164-65; establishment,
160-69; implementation, 178-80;
model, 171-95; motivation in, 161-
62; psychology, 164-65; selection,
161-62; self management, 165-70;
technical difficulties, 160
visionary leadership, 112-13
volatility in organizations, 20

work patterns, x, 138-39

About the Author

Lyndon Pugh has been a library manager in the academic sector, and a trainer and teacher of librarians, for thirty-five years. For a little over half of this time, he was Head of Learning Resources at the University of Wales Institute in Cardiff. Educated at the University of Wales Aberystwyth, he has a B.A. degree in English Literature, and for his M.A. degree he researched the poetry of R. S. Thomas. His M.Phil. research was on the topic of innovative management in libraries and learning resources. He has worked as a trainer and consultant throughout Europe, and from 1994 until 2000 was heavily involved in delivering management training for librarians in Eastern Europe and the former Soviet Union. He has written training and learning material for a number of organizations and has carried out research into organizational change in information services. He has also written on this topic and many other library management issues. Formerly the managing editor of *Ariadne*, a parallel print and Web journal that reports and comments on the development of electronic and digital libraries, he is now managing editor of *MultiMedia Information and Technology*. He also teaches management in the Department of Information Studies at the University of Wales Aberystwyth. He has recently completed a research project into organizational change in hybrid libraries, sponsored by the Library and Information Research Group of the Chartered Institute of Library and Information Professionals and Elsevier.